Writing at Work

Writing at Work

How to create effective business documents

Alan Barker

Published in 2003 by
Spiro Press
17–19 Rochester Row
London SW1P 1LA
Telephone: +44 (0)870 400 1000

© Spiro Press 2003

ISBN 1 84439 003 9

First published by The Industrial Society 1999

Reprinted: 2000, 2001, 2003
Ref: 6246.JC.3.2003

British Library Cataloguing-in-Publication Data.
A catalogue record for this book is available from the
British Library.

Spiro Press USA
3 Front Street, Suite 331
PO Box 338
Rollinsford NH 03869
USA

Typeset and printed by: JW Arrowsmith Ltd
Cover design: Sign Design

For Emma

Contents

Introduction   ix

Chapter 1 Writing for results   1

Chapter 2 Writing step by step   7

Chapter 3 Creating a message   11

Chapter 4 Organizing information   21

Chapter 5 Writing a first draft   31

Chapter 6 Effective editing   35

Chapter 7 Bringing your writing to life   61

Chapter 8 Effective layout   71

Chapter 9 Memos and e-mails   77

Chapter 10 Letters   87

Chapter 11 Reports   97

Chapter 12 Instructions and procedures   109

Chapter 13 Agendas and minutes   115

Chapter 14 Managing others' writing   125

Appendix A: The parts of speech   137

Appendix B: Sentence construction   139

Appendix C: Bones of contention   141

Appendix D: Words often confused   149

Appendix E: Some notes on dictation   153

Appendix F: Where to go from here   155

Introduction

At a glance

Every chapter starts with a box like this. It contains a summary of the material covered in that part of the book. Use these boxes to remind you of the ideas in each chapter.

You've picked up this book because you want your writing to be effective. Effective writing helps to get things done. It presents information succinctly and gives a professional impression. If you want your business documents to be more successful, then this book is for you.

We are writing more than ever at work. In many organizations, managers now have their own personal computers and have lost secretarial support. Secretaries themselves are taking on wider responsibilities. New working relationships and project management generate more paperwork. And the demand continues to grow: for e-mails, faxes, letters, reports, minutes, agendas, instructions, standard operating procedures, marketing copy, newsletters, leaflets, notices, etc.

Writing effectively is perhaps the most demanding work we do. It is both a complicated technical skill and a subtle creative activity. Putting together a clear memo can be more complicated than setting up a spreadsheet; constructing a convincing report is harder than analysing ten pages of statistics. Worst of all, we can never check a business document for absolute correctness. There is never one right way to write anything.

It's no wonder that so many people lack confidence as business writers. Few of us have learnt the essentials of effective writing. The standards and techniques that we are taught at school or college are not always appropriate at work. A letter to a customer or a project update is not like an essay or assignment; they are different kinds of document, and must be written differently.

We all know effective writing when we see it. It says exactly what the writer wants to say; nothing gets in the way. Above all, an effective document gets results.

Writing well at work is not a mysterious gift. Of course, you will need to use your imagination; but you can develop the ability to write effectively as a skill. Your task is to communicate clear messages to the people who need to read them. A good writer tackles the job step by step. This book will help you to do just that.

The boxes

> You will find boxes like this throughout the book. Each box contains essential practical information at each stage of producing a working document: guiding principles, key questions, triggers for thinking and worked examples. You could extract the boxes from the book and use them, in order, as a potted guide to effective writing.

This book is the culmination of some eight years' work teaching writing skills for The Industrial Society. My thanks to Mary Turner and Paul Brollo for their stimulating and friendly conversations, and to other Society advisers and associates who have helped me to develop my own ideas.

I am happy, too, to acknowledge the influence of Barbara Minto: we have never met, but *The Pyramid Principle* continues to inspire and clarify.

Finally, I express my warm thanks to all the many hundreds of business writers I have met on training courses and coaching sessions. They, more than anyone else, have taught me what we need to do to create effective writing, and they have shown me how satisfying it can be to see the investment of hard work on a business document paid back in practical results.

CHAPTER 1

Writing for results

> ### At a glance
> At work, we write to get results. Communication is creating shared understanding. The best way to do this is to hold a conversation. Sharing our understanding by writing is not nearly so easy.
>
> Good writers work hard to make reading as easy as possible. The three golden rules of effective writing are:
> * use words your reader will recognize easily
> * construct straightforward sentences
> * make your point, then support it,
>
> Functional writing has a job to do. It:
> * delivers a clear message
> * is supported by coherent information
> * is expressed in clear language.
>
> You don't always need to put it in writing. Use conversation to start a new business relationship, to deliver a sensitive message or to get immediate feedback. Use writing when you need a permanent record, when the information is complicated or when you want to copy the same message to many readers. Writing well begins with the decision to write.

At work, we write to get results. That's the most important idea in this book. Whenever you write, you are communicating with somebody to achieve some practical outcome. Hence my use of the phrase 'functional writing'.

Communication is creating shared understanding. We tend to think of communicating as the process of sending and receiving information, but the process is only a means to an end. *Communication* belongs to the same family of words as *community, communist* and *communion*. All of these words relate to the word *common*, meaning 'shared'. Until we have shared information with someone, we haven't communicated it. And, to share it, the sender and the receiver must understand it in the same way.

The easiest way to create shared understanding is to hold a conversation. Conversation is a dynamic of speaking and listening. It's a verbal dance: the word means 'moving around with'. Participants in a conversation respond to each others' contributions, move by move: they can change direction, focus on one part of the information or pull out to create a wider view. By asking questions and listening to the answers, they can check that understanding is being truly shared. Physical gestures, tone of voice and body language can enrich the shared meaning. The great advantage of conversation is its *speed*: we can communicate a lot of information quickly.

Sharing our understanding by writing is not so easy. Most of the advantages of conversation disappear. Compared to speaking and listening, writing and reading are slow and inefficient. A document isn't dynamic; it's static. Your reader can't ask it a question; it can't reply. Misunderstandings can arise, and, if they do, you're not there to help. Worst of all, you can't even be certain the reader will read it.

Good writers try to make reading as easy as possible. Reading, after all, is hard work. It involves:
- recognizing the words
- understanding how they fit together into sentences
- working out the relationship between the sentences.

Problems at any stage will make reading more difficult. Your readers will find the task simpler if you use words they can recognize and construct sentences that are not too complicated.

Explaining the relationship between sentences is probably the single most important part of writing clearly. Readers can read only one sentence at a time. They will assume that you have put them in a certain order to support some point you're making. Tell them what the point is, and everything will fit together in the reader's mind just as it does in yours. If you don't make your point first, the reader will look for one – and, because we all think differently, they will probably find a different one and miss the point you're trying to make.

They may not see any relationship at all between the sentences and give up reading in disgust. Look through the rest of this book to see what I mean. Every chapter opens with a box containing all the main points. I have tried to open every paragraph by making a point in a single sentence. Throughout, my aim has been to make reading as easy as possible.

The three golden rules of effective writing

Use words your reader will recognize easily
Construct straightforward sentences
Make your point, then support it

Functional writing

Functional writing has a job to do. It has a practical purpose. Of course, all writing has some sort of purpose. A novel's purpose is to entertain; the purpose of a history book is to explain and enlighten. But neither are strictly functional, because the books' purposes aren't practical: the writers don't want us to *act* as a result of reading. The more practical the purpose, the more functional the writing.

Purpose or subject: *example*

Don't confuse your document's purpose with its subject. Suppose you were writing about a new piece of equipment. You could write about it in many ways. The way you choose will depend on your purpose. What do you want your document to do? Possible objectives include:
• justifying the cost of buying it
• comparing it with similar products
• telling the reader how to operate it
• listing the options for using it
• detailing its technical specifications
• explaining how it fits into an existing network or system.
Each purpose will generate a completely different document. The document will only be useful if it addresses the purpose clearly.

A functional document:
- delivers a clear message
  - supported with coherent information
  - expressed in clear language.

Functional writing works by delivering a *message*. A message, by definition, is useful. It has a specific, practical reason for being sent. Effective messages always promote action. They must always be targeted at a specific readership. Good functional writing sends a message that is immediately clear to its target reader.

A functional document supports messages, if necessary, with coherent information. The information in a functional document must be *necessary* and *recognizable*. Information is necessary if it helps the reader understand the message in more detail; it's recognizable when the reader can easily understand and use it. Information is whatever the reader needs to know – not whatever you want to say.

Functional writing expresses its messages and information in *clear language*. Your reader is busy, and doesn't want to spend time interpreting what you are saying. The document should make sense at first reading.

Why write?

You don't always need to put it in writing. Don't be seduced into writing when a conversation would do the job better. And, when the average cost of a business letter is at least £25, it pays to ask whether putting it on paper is cost-effective.

Writing is probably *not* the best way to communicate when:
- you are starting a new relationship with a colleague, manager, staff member or customer
- you have a sensitive message that could easily be misunderstood
- your information is ambiguous, incomplete, private or confidential
- you need immediate feedback or action.

Writing *is* useful when:
- you need a permanent record – for legal, contractual, administrative or 'political' reasons
- the information is complicated – so that you can take the time to organize it clearly and the reader has time to digest it, re-read or refer to it

- you want to copy the same message to many readers — although this advantage is increasingly being abused by writers of e-mails who 'cc' everybody they can think of instead of limiting distribution to those who need to read it.

It may be useful to write to somebody who is never available to talk to — although there is no guarantee that they will notice your memo or e-mail amongst the hundreds of others they may receive that day. Writing also has a certain authority that talking lacks. A letter may get action more easily than a phone call because it looks more 'official' or 'serious'.

Writing well, then, begins with the decision to write. If you've decided that you have to write it down, and that a conversation is impossible or inappropriate, you must work out how to produce the document that will do the job for you. You must write as efficiently as possible, because time is always short; and you need to be able to check that you're asking the most useful questions.

The next chapter looks at the writing process as a whole, before looking at each stage in turn.

CHAPTER 2

Writing step by step

At a glance

Functional writing is best tackled systematically. Think of constructing a document, rather than simply writing it. Constructing a useful document involves:
- creating a message
- organizing information
- writing a first draft
- editing the draft.

Nothing is more important than your document's message. The information in the document is whatever the reader needs to know to understand your message in more detail.

Write the first draft in your own voice, without interruption (if possible) and without editing.

Rewriting is the only way to improve your writing. The language you use is like a window through which the reader can see your meaning. Editing is like cleaning the window. It is potentially endless. Your aim is not perfection but improvement.

Functional writing is best done systematically. Every writer faces the temptation to do everything at once: thinking what to say, in what order, and how to say it. This is a recipe for disaster: it produces confusion, frustration and a garbled mess. Like any other complicated technical task, writing is best approached step by step.

Think in terms of *constructing* a functional document, rather than simply writing it. Your document has a job to do; you must design and build it to do the job.

Design and build

If you were building a table, you would begin with some basic questions.

Who will be using the table?

What for?

What design would be most useful to them?

What materials would they prefer?

How much are they willing to pay?

How many should it seat?

Any special equipment or attachments?

Any design constraints?

Consistency with other features in the room?

When is the table needed?

You can probably think of other questions. You would need to talk to your client to answer many of them clearly. Their answers would influence how you designed the table.

Ask similar questions when designing a business document. How would the questions about the table translate into questions about that document?

The construction process has four steps:

- creating a message
- organizing information
- writing a first draft
- editing the draft.

Try to keep the stages separate. If you can take breaks between them, so much the better: you will be able to review your work with fresh eyes. It can also be useful to ask a colleague for help between stages, to offer their thoughts on your plan or on the first draft itself.

Creating a message

Nothing is more important than your document's message. This is what you want to say to your reader: the point you are making. If you have no message for your reader, there's no point in writing.

To work out your message, concentrate on your reader and what you want to tell them. Beware of thinking too much about *information*: how accurate, complete and detailed it is. Visualize the reader and what they need to know.

Organizing information

The information in your document is whatever the reader needs to know to understand the message in more detail. It is *not* whatever you may want to tell them.

To be understood, information must have a structure. The structure should be clear, familiar and useful. For example, if the reader can *see* three key points without searching for them, the structure is clear. If they are in an order that makes sense to the reader, the structure is familiar. If the reader can see *why* they are in that order, the structure is useful.

Of course, your message may not need any supporting information. If it can do its job alone, so much the better.

You may want to *outline* your document. An outline is a 'blueprint' of the document, mapping out its message, main points and structure. The outline forms the basis for the first draft. Just as with a design drawing, you can also show the outline to your prospective reader to check that the document will be useful.

Writing a first draft

You can only write a first draft once. Your task at this stage is only to write. You can't get it right first time, so don't try. Simply write the draft, taking care to keep to your outline or plan.

- Get going. Don't wait for inspiration to strike. Starting to write is a lot easier if you have a plan or outline in front of you. If you have no plan, you could begin by writing whatever comes into your head – even if it's nonsense. Keep writing. Before long, something meaningful will start to appear.
- Write in your own voice. Imagine holding a conversation with your reader. How would you *say* what you want to say? If necessary, speak the words aloud and transcribe them directly to the page. Use a tape recorder or dictaphone if you wish.

- Write without interruption. This can be hard to achieve: open-plan offices, telephones and meetings all get in the way. Try to allocate specific times when you do nothing but write – even if these are only short periods (your outline will help you keep on track). Some times of day may be better than others: early morning, just before lunch, late evening. Can you manage your time to make space for writing?
- Eliminate as many distractions as you can. Clear your mind, your action list and your in-tray; do what must be done now and put off what you can. Try to resolve any issue that nags at you, so that it doesn't worry you as you write.
- Write without editing. Don't stop to check or correct; finish the first draft and print it out. On long documents, you may wish to complete a whole section before editing.

Editing the draft

Rewriting is the only way to improve your writing. The language you use is like a window through which the reader can see what you mean. Editing the text is like cleaning the window: the aim is to produce language that is transparently clear.

- Check that what you've written makes sense.
- Remove what you don't need.
- Polish what is left to make it as clear as possible.

Editing is potentially endless. There can never be a perfect version of any document (just as there can never be a perfect design of table). Aim, not for perfection, but for improvement. Time, of course, is always a limiting factor. If you edit only a single sentence, the document will have improved. Editing, like the other parts of the writing process, is best done step by step.

CHAPTER 3

Creating a message

> ### *At a glance*
> The message is the most important part of the document. To work out the message, ask 'Who is my reader?' and 'What is my objective?' Your message expresses your objective to your reader.
>
> Focus on the reader, not on the information. Ask some key questions to help you address the reader more directly. Think about 'reader benefit'. What is the document worth to the reader? What will the reader do after reading it?
>
> You must know what you want the document to do. Give your document a single function: one job to do.
>
> Imagine holding a conversation with the reader. Your message is the single most important point you would say to them. There is never a single 'correct' message for any document. Only you will know whether your chosen message is what you want to say.

The message is the most important part of a functional document. If the reader doesn't get the message, there's no point in writing. If you want to get the message across, spend a little time working out what message you want to give.

To work out your message, ask:

- 'Who is my reader?'
- 'What is my objective?'

Your message will express your objective to your reader. It will say what you wish to say to the reader to achieve your goal.

Who is my reader?

Focus on the reader, not on the information.

An effective document is written for the reader – not for the writer. It will be useful only if the reader finds it useful. Many business documents fail because writers concentrate on the information they want to give, rather than on what the reader needs to know. Imagine that you are the reader. What would you want to know? What would be interesting or useful?

Reader: *key questions*

Asking these key questions will help you address your readers more directly.

- Who are they? How many are there? Do you know their names? It may be worth the effort to find out. What are their backgrounds and roles in the organization?
- What do you want them to *do*? Are they able to take the action you want? Your document may be wasted if the wrong person reads it.
- What do they need to know? What do they want to hear? There may be a conflict between the two.
- What do they already know? A colleague, a member of the public, an expert or a child: what they understand will determine how you address them.
- How well do they know you? Does the situation have a history? Your organization may have a particular public image or reputation. How could you influence your readers positively?

You may know the reader so well that you hardly need to pause to consider these questions. If you are writing to complete strangers you may need to do a little detective work – or guessing – to picture them accurately in your mind. Your reader may not have English as a first language. More and more customers and colleagues are abroad or come from diverse cultural backgrounds. Your message must be as clear as possible to avoid misunderstanding or offence.

Reader benefit

Your document has value only if the reader can see its value. When starting to read your document, your reader will ask two urgent questions:

- 'What's in it for me?' – Why should I bother to read this? How does this document affect me? What am I expected to do with it? What effect will it have on my work?
- 'So what?' – Why are you telling me this? What point are you making? How does it relate to everything else you're telling me? Think about reader benefit. What is the document worth to the reader, in terms of time and effort?

What readers don't want

Thinking about what readers *don't* want is as useful as thinking about what they need.

They probably don't want to read anything. Think of how *you* feel as you sift through 120 irrelevant e-mails – or when another weighty report lands on your desk. What could you say that will motivate the reader to read on? How can you make reading *easier* for them?

They don't want lots of information. Most of us receive far more information than we need or can deal with. Your readers won't thank you for adding to the problem. Give them only what they need to do the job. Anything else is surplus to requirements.

They don't want a story. Very few managers read business documents from beginning to end. Readers don't want to be entertained; they want to *use* the document. Stories tend to be about the past; a useful business document will probably be about what to do in the future.

Action point

What will happen as a result of your document?

The action point is the first or next step that the reader (or writer) needs to take to fulfil the document's purpose. The action point is specific: dates, times, places, names, numbers.

- What action is required? By whom? When? Where?

- What information is relevant to the action point?
- What does the reader need to know to carry out the action?
- What do they already know about this?
- What else do they need to know?

  The action point should indicate:
- what action is to be taken (at your end or the reader's)
- when it is to be taken
- who is responsible for taking it.

Some documents may seem not to have obvious action points. Regular weekly reports about your department's activities, monthly papers on market trends or sales figures, project updates: it's hard sometimes to see what readers *do* with these documents. Undoubtedly they need this information; otherwise, they wouldn't ask for it. Discuss this with them. Why do they demand these regular updates? How do they use the information? Could you organize or edit the material so that it's easier to use?

What do you want your reader to do?

Different actions require different kinds of understanding. Look through this list of possible actions and see which is most suitable for your document. You may be able to think of something that works better for your needs.

After reading this document, I want my reader to:

Attend a meeting	Fill in a form
Give me answers	Stop complaining
Speak to a colleague	Buy my product
Take a number of steps	Provide input
Give me their opinion	Call me
Complete a timesheet	Order goods
Consider applications	Agree with me
Sign a cheque	Release funds
Allocate resources	Put it right
Investigate a problem	Gather information
Give me feedback	Prepare a presentation
Join the team	Finish the job

Other readers

Many business documents have more than one reader. These are the 'cc' names, the distribution list or the people who get copies 'for information only'.

Your primary reader will put the document to immediate use. If the primary reader doesn't read it, there is no point in writing it. If you have more than one primary reader, there must be *one* purpose that binds them together. Perhaps they all need to agree to the proposal; perhaps they are all users or customers.

Secondary readers will not use the document but may need to know that you've sent it. A colleague may need a record so that they can pick up the matter in your absence; a senior manager may need to keep track of what's happening in the department; your line manager may need to authorize a letter before you send it.

Many business documents have too many secondary readers. E-mail, in particular, makes it all too easy to download lots of copies. Some people seem to consider large distribution lists as some sort of status symbol. Copying documents to whole populations is a major cause of information overload: don't do it.

Primary and secondary readers

- Who is your primary reader?
- How many? Why are they all primary?
- What do you want them to do?
- What do they need to know to do it?

- Who are your secondary readers?
- How will they use the document?
- Do they all need to see it?
- What would happen if they didn't see the document? If the answer is 'nothing', why are you sending a copy?

'What is my objective?'

You must know what you want the document to do. You might call this the document's objective, aim, goal or purpose. I like the word *function*.

Two key principles govern a document's function.

- It must relate to the primary reader: what you want them to do; what they need to do; how they will use the document.
- It should be as specific as possible. The more you can pinpoint its function, the clearer the document will be.

Above all, your document should have a *single* function. Many business documents fail because they try to tackle too many objectives at once. You cannot create a clear, useful document if it has more than one function.

Finding it may not be easy. Your primary reader may not have given you a clear brief. A customer's letter may be confused; a manager may say no more than: 'Write me a report about ...' The reader may ask for several things: 'Give me the available options, recommend one and tell me why so I can justify it to the Board.' In these cases, you must choose a single function for the document. If you were answering a letter of complaint, what would you want your letter to do? To express sympathy? To explain how you will put things right? To disclaim all responsibility? Only you can choose.

The document's function

Writing down the function of the document will help you clarify your thinking and work out what you want the document to do. If you are asking your document to *inform, advise, tell, communicate* or *present*, ask whether you can make the function more specific and less general. This will help you later, when you come to organizing information. The content of the document will be dictated by its function; information will be organized differently to achieve different actions or outcomes.
Here are some possible functions for the document you are writing. Try them out and see which is most suitable. You may be able to think of another that fits better.

The document's function – *continued*

The aim of this document is to:

Persuade	Sell	Ask
Complain	Highlight	Identify action needed
Recommend	Respond to a complaint	List items wanted
Instruct	Update	Summarize
Ratify	Confirm	Describe
Clarify	Invite	Propose
Compare	Justify	Explain
Argue	Highlight	Outline

If your document seems to have more than one function, pick the most important one and regard it as the document's overall task. Other tasks or functions should contribute to it.

'What do I want to say?'

Your message expresses your objective to your reader. It isn't a title or a heading, or an explanation of what you are doing in the document. Your message is the single most important thing you need to say to achieve your objective.

Constructing a message

Imagine holding a conversation with your reader. What is the single most important thing you would say to them to achieve your purpose? Write it down: that is your message. Now imagine speaking the message to the reader face to face, exactly as you've written it. Would it make sense? Is it appropriate? What kind of response would it get?

The message should:

- be a fully grammatical sentence (not just a heading)
- make a single point
- contain no more than about 15 words
- express your purpose (and not describe it)
- be action-centred (about doing something)
- make complete sense, and not refer to something outside itself

- be interesting to the reader.

If the message tells your reader something new, it will be more likely to be interesting. If it is interesting, the reader should want to read on.

Constructing a message: *example*

Imagine you are writing to a customer to introduce a new service. What message could you give?
Here are some examples that break the key rules for messages.

New Payment Facility
This is not a fully grammatical sentence; merely a heading.

Our new direct debit facility is easy to use and will speed up your payments.
This message makes two points, not one.

Our new, state of the art direct debit facility will allow you to make payments more quickly and comfortably than ever before.
Too long: more than 15 words.

This leaflet explains our new direct debit facility.
I would like to explain our new direct debit facility to you.
Both of these messages describe the writer's purpose, rather than expressing it.

Our new payment facility is one of the most advanced in Europe.
Not action-centred for the customer.

This will help you make speedier payments.
Not self-contained: 'this' refers to something outside the message.

Your message simply makes the single most important point you want to make to the reader.

You can now pay us by direct debit.
This message fulfils all the criteria for effectiveness. And it's interesting: it should make the customer stop and take notice; it is new information; it's easily understood; and – with luck – the reader will want to read on.

There is never a single correct message for any document. Only you will know whether your chosen message is what you want to say. Take time to formulate the message that says exactly what you want to say. That way, you will be better prepared to find and structure the information to support it.

CHAPTER 4

Organizing information

At a glance

Supporting information helps the reader understand your message in more detail.

Organizing information means:
- breaking it into a small number of pieces
- shaping it clearly.

Include only what the reader needs to know – not everything you know.

Make your point, then support it.

Create an imaginary conversation with the reader. Use the conversation to generate answers to the questions provoked by your message. Write up the points you have made as an outline. This is the plan of your document. It includes your message, and the supporting key points. Everything is written in sentences. Creating an outline makes writing the first draft easier. It shows you clearly what points to make and allows you to alter the structure or emphasis of key points without having to alter lots of text.

Supporting information helps the reader to understand your message in more detail. Any information that explains the message further is useful. Everything else is waffle.

Information is whatever the reader can easily understand. You must keep the reader 'tuned in'. It's important to keep the signal clear, making sure that it isn't obscured by interference or noise. Organizing information is the skill of presenting it so that the signal remains clear.

Organizing information means breaking it into a manageable number of pieces. The mind can only hold so many pieces at once. The easiest number of pieces to remember, of course, is one. Beyond that, the biggest number is about seven. If we confront more than this number, we either lose track or begin to group the pieces into categories. About seven categories is about the most we can manage at once.

Organizing information also means shaping it clearly. Somebody once defined understanding as shape recognition: we understand information because we recognize the way it's structured. Different people understand information in different ways. Just as you have created a message for the reader, so you must now create a reader-centred structure. Will your reader understand it the way you do? To the same level of detail? From the same point of view? In the same language? If the reader can see the shape of your information clearly, they will understand it. Adding detail will always risk making the overall shape less clear.

Organizing information: *first questions*

- What do you want the reader to do?
- What does the reader need to know beyond the message itself?
- What would be the best way of shaping this material?
- How much do they already know?
- What do you know that they don't?
- How much of what you know does the reader need to know?

Information is whatever the reader *needs* to know. Your reader will assume that you've ordered the information to support a point. If you give the point first, the reader will know how to order the information. If you don't, they may order it differently, or worse, miss the point, in which case you are both wasting your time.

The clearest way to organize information is to give the reader your message first, then present a few key points to support it. Each key point might then split up again into a few sub-points. This top-down approach helps the reader to understand the structure of the information, because you have presented the summarizing idea before presenting the individual bits of information being summarized.

Imagining a conversation

A simple way to organize information is to create an imaginary conversation. The most useful conversation would be the one that allows you to display the structure of your information clearly. Imagine that your message generates a question in the reader's mind. You can then structure the supporting information as responses to that question.

The message can generate an imaginary conversation in four main ways. It may provoke:

- no questions
- several questions
- one question with one answer
- one question with several answers.

We'll look at each of these possibilities in turn.

The message provokes no questions

Some messages don't provoke a question.

I'll be in the hotel lobby at 8 o'clock.

Please fill in and return the enclosed form by next Friday.

Do we need the Marroflex disk at the presentation?

Because the reader doesn't ask a question, you don't need to say any more. These messages can form one-line memos or e-mails.

Whether these are truly one-liners, of course, depends on your relationship with the reader. Presumably the first message is part of a pre-existing arrangement and needs no further explanation. The second message may provoke the question 'Why?': you would then need to explain the reasons for your request. The last message, being itself a question, should provoke an answer, not a question. The writer assumes that the reader knows what 'the Marroflex disk' is (and what 'the presentation' means).

The message provokes several questions

A message that provokes several questions at once is probably not as strong as it might be. If your reader could respond to your message in several ways, you may not be making your point clearly enough. Rethink your message by returning to the key questions: 'What do I want to achieve?' and 'Who is my reader?'

Strengthening your message: *example*

Here is a message that is not as strong as it could be.

You must follow the new procedure for disposing of paper waste. The reader might ask: 'Why must we do this?' or 'What is the new procedure?' You could rethink the message by asking what you want to achieve in the document. If your objective is to instruct the reader in the new procedure, a stronger message might be:

We have a new procedure for disposing of paper waste.

If you need to convince management that they should adopt the new procedure, the message might read:

We should dispose of paper waste in a better way.

If you feel that you need to do both – persuade the reader of the benefits of the new procedure *and* tell them what to do – you might separate the messages and create two documents: a procedure, and a covering note outlining the reasons for change.

The message provokes one question with one answer

If your message provokes only one question, you may have only one answer. Call this your *key point*, to distinguish it from your message.

- Look at your message and ask what question it is likely to provoke in the reader's mind. You should be able to limit yourself to one of three possible questions.

Is the memo [?] (handwritten)

Why?, How? or *Which?*

- Write down the answer to that question. This is your key point. Write it *as a sentence* after your message.
- Does your key point itself provoke an imaginary question? If so, write the answer. *Remember to keep the reader in mind all the time.* Only answer the questions you can imagine your reader asking. Carry on giving answers until you imagine the questions stopping. Make sure that each point provokes only one question at a time: one of *why*, *how* or *which*. Try to limit yourself to about six questions and answers in all.
- If necessary, add an action point: what is to be done, by whom, when and where.

Creating a simple structure using questions and answers: *example*

Here is a simple memo from an IT department to system users, created from a short sequence of questions and answers. The message reads:

We will be altering our helpdesk arrangements for Thursday afternoon only.

This provokes the question 'How?' Your answer to the question is your key point.

From 1400 until 1700 only, the helpline extension number will be 1243.

This may in turn provoke the question 'Why?' If you feel that the reader will ask this question, you should answer it. You might call this next point a *minor point*, because, from the reader's point of view, it is less important than the key point.

This temporary arrangement allows us to install new software.

This point may now provoke the question 'Which software?' – but users are unlikely to ask this question, so you choose not to answer it. You add an action point.

At 1700, the helpdesk returns to its usual extension number: 8765.

The message provokes one question with several answers

You can develop the pattern of questions and answers to create a structure that will display more complicated information simply. The question provoked by the message is a clue to the structure of the information you need to provide.

- Ask what question your message provokes in the reader's mind. Limit yourself strictly to one of three possible questions. *Why?, How?* or *Which?*
- Write down your answers to the question. These are your *key points*. You should have between two and six key points. They should all be sentences, not just headings: you can only make a point by writing a sentence.
- *All the key points must be of the same kind.* They must all answer the single question provoked by the message. The key points will be of three broad kinds:
  - reasons, causes or benefits (answering the question 'Why?')
  - procedures, steps in a procedure or ways in which something happens ('How?')
  - items, categories or factors to be considered ('Which?').
- Put the key points into an order. Ask *why they are in that order.* Your reader may have asked you for a specific order of items; it might be discourteous not to oblige. Otherwise, the order of the key points may be:
  - chronological or procedural (first, second, third)
  - structural (breaking a whole into parts: points, sections, blocks or areas)
  - comparative (biggest to smallest, most important to least important)
  - deductive (steps in a logical argument).

Building a pyramid: *example*

Structuring the document in this way is like building a pyramid – from the top down. At the top is the message; below it, on the *keyline*, are the key points that support it.

You will find it easier to see the structure of your information if you actually draw a pyramid made up of boxes containing your message and key points.

Here are three examples of simple pyramids. The first is an internal memo.

The next is a customer letter.

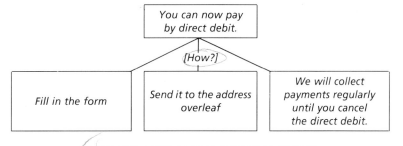

The last is a procedural e-mail.

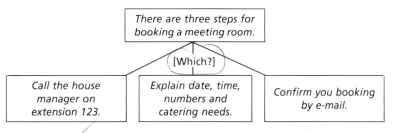

If the points on the keyline provoke no more questions, the pyramid is complete.

Producing an outline

Write up the structure you have created as an *outline*. This is the plan of the document on a single sheet of paper. It translates the pyramid you've drawn into the linear structure of text.

An outline is the blueprint or plan of your document. It isn't a first draft. It won't include all the information you wish to include, or every point you want to make. It shows you the shape of your thinking in simplified form. It includes your message, and all the key points you want to make to support it. Everything is written in sentences.

Creating an outline is useful because:
- it shows you clearly what points to make
- you can alter the structure or emphasis of key points without having to alter lots of text.

Producing an outline forces you to clarify your thinking *before* writing. It is sometimes useful as a discussion document: show it to the reader or 'client' to check that the document is what they want.

How to write an outline

1. Place your message at the top of a piece of paper.
2. Add all your key points *as single sentences* spaced down the page. You should have no more than about six or seven. None of your sentences should make more than a single point. None should be longer than about 15 words.
3. Avoid writing headings. Expressing your ideas in sentences forces you to make points and to be clear in your thinking. Sentences allow you to express key points; headings do not.
4. You may want to number your key points to help display the structure of your information.
5. If necessary, add an action point: what is to be done, by whom, when and where.
6. Check your outline by asking:
   - Is the message appropriate to the [primary] reader?
   - Does it express your purpose?
   - What question does the message provoke ('Why?', or 'How?' 'Which?')

– Do all the key point sentences answer that question?
– Are all the key points of the same kind?
– What principle governs the order of your key points?
– Is anything important missing?
– Is this the document you want to write?

From pyramid to outline: *example*

Translate the pyramid into a simple outline by putting the message at the top of a piece of paper, and each key point on the keyline as a separate sentence spaced down the page. Add an action point at the end, and the outline is complete.

We need to hold a sales team meeting. *Why*	You can now pay by direct debit. *How*	There are three steps for booking a meeting room. *when*
We need to agree new territory boundaries.	Fill in the form.	Call the house manager on extension 123.
Everybody needs briefing on the Hayward range.	Send it to the address overleaf.	Explain date, time, numbers and catering needs.
The sales director wants to explain future European strategy.	We will collect payments until you cancel the direct debit.	Confirm your booking by e-mail.
Please let me know your availability during the week beginning 2 February.	If you have any queries, please call us free on:	Please try to make your booking at least 24 hours in advance.

An outline makes writing the first draft easier. You now know what key points you want to make. You can start writing anywhere in the document; you don't have to begin at the beginning. If you are interrupted, you can pick up the threads more easily. You can pace yourself, by being able to see how much you've produced and how much is left to write.

CHAPTER 5

Writing a first draft

> **At a glance**
> **Write your first draft:**
> - **without editing**
> - **quickly**
> - **in your own voice**
> - **without interruption.**

Having planned your document, you can write it.

Producing a first draft, though, is sometimes easier said than done. The conditions need to be right. Most professional writers can only work by establishing a solid routine. Many have special rooms and furniture for writing. Few business writers are as privileged. However, you may be able to improve the circumstances in which you write.

Be guided by these broad principles:
- write without editing
- write quickly
- write in your own voice
- try to write without interruption.

Write without editing

You can only write a first draft once. All the work to alter and improve the first draft is rewriting or editing. Distinguish between these two activities, and separate them. The objective of writing a first draft is to produce 'work in progress': text that you can work with. The aim of editing is to improve the draft by making it clearer.

Don't try to get it right first time. Nobody ever produced a perfect version at the first attempt. Wordprocessing software makes editing supremely simple, and it's easy to be seduced into editing as you go. Resist the temptation as much as possible. You will tend to get stuck and waste time.

Write quickly

Don't ponder too long, or choose your words too carefully. At this stage, it's more important to keep going. Leave gaps if necessary. Aim for a natural flow, in which words follow one another easily.

Write in your own voice

Expressing yourself in your own way will help you say what you mean more exactly. And, if your reader can 'hear' your voice, reading will be easier and more pleasurable. Speaking in your own voice forms the basis of an individual and interesting written style.

Professionalism in modern business writing means speaking personally to your reader. Don't be tempted to stifle your voice when you write. You may be under pressure to conform to 'corporate style'. It's easy to be influenced by colleagues or managers and you may simply copy what you see written around you.

Writing in your own voice doesn't quite mean 'writing as you speak'. Spoken sentences tend to be much longer than written sentences should be. Listeners will usually tolerate a certain amount of extra language. But reading is harder work than listening, and a very few unnecessary words can quickly become 'waffle'.

With your outline in front of you, imagine speaking to your reader directly. Try to discipline what you would say, by imagining that time is short or that the situation is slightly formal. Take each keypoint and add any other information that you would add to explain it further. Continue until you've dealt with that point as much as you need. Then deliberately move to the next keypoint, probably starting a new paragraph.

Try to listen to the voice inside your head as you write. At its best, the effect is like writing from dictation.

Try to write without interruption

This is a serious problem. Meetings, open-plan offices and the telephone conspire to destroy concentration. You may be lucky: your organization may have set aside 'quiet rooms' with computer terminals but no phones, where you can work in peace. If not, finding the time and space to write can seem impossible. But you will be able to write well only if you are quiet, comfortable, free from distractions and able to hear the voice inside your head.

- Is there a time of day when you are in the best mood to write? It may be first thing in the morning, or at the end of the day when the telephones stop ringing. Can you organize your time to be able to write at these peak times?
- Can you write at home? This option can make for better and more efficient work.
- Your physical condition affects your writing ability. Writing is notoriously sedentary – unless you can dictate while jogging. Pay attention to your posture and breathing. Take regular breaks. Exercise regularly: the link between physical and mental agility is well established. Physical work is particularly beneficial to break writer's block. You will write better if you are relaxed but alert. Review the comfort of your chair and the quality of the light by which you work.
- Pay attention to what you eat and drink (and when). Writing after a heavy meal, for example, is obviously unwise.

Once your first draft is complete, print it out and put it aside. Leave it for as long as possible before editing. Polishing your own draft is much more difficult than editing someone else's work. If you try to edit immediately after writing, you will miss ambiguities and obvious errors. If you return to your document after a break, you have a much better chance of seeing what you've written with an innocent eye.

CHAPTER 6

Effective editing

At a glance

Edit your document to make it easier to read. Use plain English. Editing is about making choices. Try to take a break before starting; ask for a second opinion; edit hard copy. Edit systematically, working in order on:

- paragraphs
- sentences
- words.

Paragraphs show the shape of your thinking and make the page more inviting. They are as long as they need to be. Use *topic sentences* to summarize paragraphs. Bullet points can lighten a paragraph; use them sparingly.

Sentences express ideas. The strongest sentences are well constructed. Strengthen weak sentences by:

- cutting up long sentences into separate sentences
- separating multiple sentences
- cutting down long sentences
- rebuilding complicated sentences
- making non-sentences whole
- finding strong subjects and main verbs.

Prefer shorter words to longer ones. Work on:

- passive verbs
- abstract nouns
- unnecessary words.

The aim of editing is to make the first draft easier to read. The words on the page should never get in the way of your meaning.

The reader should never have to stop and wonder what you're saying. Language is like a window through which your reader sees what you mean. Editing is like polishing the window: you are aiming to make your words transparently clear.

Plain English

Plain English helps any reader to understand information at first reading. The word 'plain' suggests clarity, simplicity and honesty. Plain English speaks the truth without embellishment. It doesn't hide information behind a mass of detail, jargon or managerial gobbledegook.

Plain English doesn't offer instant or perfect solutions. What is plain to an accountant may be unclear to a biologist; what is precise in Glasgow may be ambiguous in Delhi or Toronto. What a reader understands today may mean something else in ten years' time. Pitch your language to suit the reader and the situation. The ultimate test of any functional document is whether it gets the results you want.

Plain English, then, is a code of best practice rather than a set of rigid rules. Some people fear that Plain English creates a bland, anonymous style: that it drags us all down to some lowest common denominator and impoverishes the nation's vocabulary. I think such fears are unfounded. Using Plain English helps you to find your voice. It helps you to choose from the huge range of words the language offers us, and to develop your own individual style.

Plain English: *essential guidelines*

- Make your average sentence length 15 to 20 words.
- Use only the words that your reader is most likely to understand.
- Use only as many words as you need.
- Use the strongest, clearest and most specific verbs you can.
- Say what you mean: be positive; avoid standard expressions and tired formulas.
- Punctuate accurately and simply.

(With thanks to Martin Cutts, *The Plain English Guide*, Oxford, 1995.)

Editing systematically

Editing is about making choices. It involves adding, deleting and moving text; finding new words or phrases; giving examples and checking facts. Editing is potentially endless because there is never only one way to say what you mean.

It's especially hard to edit your own writing. After all, you know what you wanted to say; this makes it harder to know whether the reader will read it the same way. To edit well, you must cultivate an innocent eye.

Take a break before editing. Set your first draft aside for a while and turn to something else. You then have a better chance of looking at the draft afresh, and seeing what you have written rather than what you thought you wrote. Taking a break also gives your unconscious mind the opportunity to make connections you may not have made consciously: new ideas, examples or facts may emerge; you will be able to see more clearly what to add, what to move and what to remove.

You could also ask for a second opinion. Give your work to a colleague who knows nothing about it, so that they can give you an objective response. They must be someone whose opinion you trust, and they must be willing to give their views without trying to take over. Editing someone else's writing is relatively easy: it's always possible to find a different way of saying something. You, the writer, must remain in charge, ready to make your own choices.

Edit systematically. Editing word by word is time-consuming and tedious. A more efficient approach is to work on separate levels, from the largest units of meaning to the smallest:

- paragraphs
- sentences
- words.

It's probably best to edit hard copy. Editing on screen is very easy, of course, but the results are often unsatisfactory. The screen itself seems to be a barrier between you and the text. Errors that are obvious on paper can disappear. The screen may only show part of a page, so that it's hard to see exactly how the printed text will look. Scribbling on paper creates physical contact between you, the pencil and the paper, which seems to make editing more effective.

Editing paragraphs

Paragraphs display the shape of your information. Paragraphs show the main ideas that you want to convey, and the relationships between them. Use a new paragraph for each new idea, key point or topic. Every time you take a step, alter your point of view or change direction in your thinking, you should start a new paragraph.

Paragraphs also make the page look more inviting. A page is less tiring to read if it isn't a solid mass of print. Paragraphs please the eye and show your reader that you've taken the trouble to organize your ideas for them.

How long should a paragraph be?

Paragraphs are as long as they need to be. There is no iron rule governing their length. Shorter paragraphs are easier to read; too many short paragraphs, though, can make your writing look choppy and incoherent. Follow these guidelines.

- Have at least three paragraphs on each page of text.
- Vary the length of the paragraphs on each page as much as possible.
- As a *rough* guide, aim for paragraphs of between three and six sentences.
- Use a short paragraph at the start of a document or section as a summary or introduction.

Of course, for maximum impact, you could write a paragraph of only one sentence.

Topic sentences

Topic sentences summarize paragraphs. A topic sentence helps you to decide what to include in the paragraph, and what to leave out. All the material in the paragraph should support the topic sentence. If the paragraph contains material that doesn't support the topic sentence, remove it; if it lacks important material that would support the topic sentence, add it.

The topic sentence should be the *first* sentence in the paragraph. In this way, you obey the fundamental rule of structuring material in functional writing: *make your point, then support it.* A topic sentence should:

- be a fully grammatical sentence
- make a single point
- contain no more than about 15 words
- say something new.

Your outline is a ready source of topic sentences. If you have written the first draft directly out of the outline, many of your paragraphs will already have topic sentences: they are the key points in the outline.

Another useful place to look for potential topic sentences is at the end of a paragraph. Very often you write a paragraph as a 'stream of consciousness': a sequence of thoughts leading to a conclusion. Because the conclusion is in fact the key point of the paragraph, you could try moving it to the start of the paragraph as a topic sentence. You can then sometimes remove some material from the paragraph and tighten it up.

Linking paragraphs together

Topic sentences should make sense in order. You should be able to read the topic sentences and understand the whole piece in summary. You can see from the topic sentences whether one paragraph follows logically from another, whether you are repeating yourself, or whether you have left out an important point.

Use link words or phrases to show the connections between paragraphs. A transition may be a single word, a phrase or even the whole topic sentence. It's important to make the links between paragraphs explicit. Don't worry that you may make your writing too obvious or simplistic. If you don't spell out the connections between paragraphs, your reader may misunderstand you.

Link words and phrases: *examples*

Use words and phrases like these in your topic sentences to show the relationship of one paragraph to another. Some you can use at the start of the topic sentence; others you can place within it.

for example	*for instance*	*because*
given that	*since*	*on account of*
that is	*such as*	*so that*
due to	*owing to*	*in order to*
for this reason	*as a result*	*therefore*
consequently	*subsequently*	*thus*
next	*then*	*before*
after	*meanwhile*	*similarly*
in the same way	*on the other hand*	*but*
although	*however*	*by comparison*
also	*too*	*as well*
as well as	*in addition to*	*besides*
in other words	*again*	*in conclusion*
in brief	*to sum up*	*at the same time*
later	*previously*	*moreover*
first, secondly, thirdly...	*likewise*	*in contrast to*
nevertheless	*on the contrary*	*alternatively*

Using key words

Key words bind a paragraph together. Certain words in your document are at the heart of what you are trying to say and do; never be afraid to repeat such key words.

Beware of using different words to express the same thing. Many people try hard to avoid repeating words in their writing. They look for *synonyms* – different words with the same meaning – often using a thesaurus to do so. Perhaps they remember a schoolteacher telling them not to repeat the same word in an essay, as a way of encouraging a wider use of vocabulary. Unfortunately, readers are often more confused than impressed by a mass of different words.

Distinguish between key words and other, less important, words. Repeat key words to reinforce your keypoints and pull the paragraph together. Repeating non-key words can be distracting.

Paragraph layout

Block paragraphs to the left and leave a single line space between each. Blocked layout (without indenting the first lines of paragraphs) looks neater, is more inviting to the reader and will make the text easier to read.

It's often useful to break a paragraph into sub-paragraphs. These are best indented as blocks within the paragraph. You might consider numbering them.

Bullet points

Bullet points can lighten a paragraph by presenting detailed information in a more digestible form. They are increasingly popular in business writing. However, they're not easy to use well.

Use bullet points sparingly. They are visually strong: the reader will almost certainly read them before anything else on the page. Indenting may make them stronger still. Using too many lists on one page destroys the effect. Take care, too, that your bullet points don't emphasize minor detail. Use them to list a *small number* of important pieces of information – as a rough guide, no more than about six.

Bullet points are a *graphic* device. Because they display information visually, they need to abide by some simple design conventions. Don't confuse these with the conventions of punctuation. Follow these guidelines to make bullet points work effectively.

Use parallel construction. Write every item in the list to the same pattern. It might be a single word, a phrase or clause, a sentence or even a short paragraph. The items may all have the same grammatical structure. For example, they might begin with infinitives, active or passive verbs, or participles.

Make full use of the 'platform'. This is the line of text that introduces the list. It may be a part of a sentence or a complete sentence. If you find that items in the list repeat elements tediously, put the repeated element into the platform instead.

Create consistency between platform and list.   If the platform is an incomplete sentence, each item in the list should be able to fit on the end and make sense. If the platform is a complete sentence, the items in the list can stand alone – but they should still be constructed in parallel.

Punctuate the list coherently.   You can punctuate bullet-pointed lists in two ways.

- If the platform is an incomplete sentence, follow it with a colon (:). Each listed item begins with a lower-case letter and may end with a semi-colon (;). The last item takes a full stop(.). You could add 'and' or 'or', as necessary, after the last semi-colon or before the last item. If you want to continue the sentence beyond the list, use a semi-colon after the last item and begin the continuation with a lower-case letter.
- If the platform is a complete sentence, finish with a full stop. If the listed items are complete sentences, use upper-case letters at the beginning of each, and full stops at the end. If any item in the list consists of more than one sentence, you *must* punctuate as sentences throughout – and ensure that your platform is a complete sentence. If the listed items aren't sentences, use upper case at the start of each, and *no* punctuation at the end.

Consider using numbers.   Numbering is useful if you want to suggest that the points must follow a certain order. The order may be dictated by process, chronology, size or priority. Any numbering will automatically suggest that the order is important; don't use numbers if order is irrelevant.

Numbers create a 'busier' visual effect. The list becomes more cluttered and therefore less effective. Arabic numbers are probably the least intrusive (1,2,3...). Decimal points, Roman numerals (I,II,III...; i,ii,iii...), and letters all create more jumble.

Icons or 'dingbats' offer an alternative to simple bullet points. Most wordprocessing packages now contain a range of visual characters to enliven lists. In some, you can even create your own. They are very strong visual markers – use them with care.

Creating bullet point lists: *example*

This passage would clearly benefit from reconstructing the list in bullet points.

Within our report we have raised a number of concerns over the lack of insurance information available to the Claims Unit, such as claims manuals, procedures for reporting fraud, benchmark averages in estimating claims for personal injuries and underwriting procedures.

The platform for the list could be an incomplete sentence.

In our report we have raised a number of concerns over the lack of information available to the Claims Unit, such as:

- *claims manuals*
- *procedures for reporting fraud*
- *benchmark averages in estimating claims for personal injuries*
- *underwriting procedures.*

Alternatively, the platform could be a complete sentence. A number in the platform sentence makes the meaning clearer.

In our report we have raised four concerns over the lack of information available to the Claims Unit:

- *claims manuals*
- *procedures for reporting fraud*
- *benchmark averages in estimating claims for personal injuries*
- *underwriting procedures.*

Editing sentences

Sentences express ideas. They make the points you want to make, and you will make those points more strongly if you use sturdy sentences.

Some sentences are difficult to read simply because they are too long. There are no rigid rules about sentence length. Modern English sentences are, on average, about 17 words long. Aim to make your own average between 15 and 20 words. Your wordprocessing software should be able to calculate average sentence length for you. Try to achieve a *maximum* sentence length, throughout the document, of 25 words.

The best sentences are well constructed. Sentences are built with *phrases*: groups of words that express a single element of meaning.

An effective sentence is well built; it makes sense at one reading; it says what's necessary *and no more*. Sentences may be poorly constructed for a number of reasons. They may straggle or be too complicated. They may be incomplete or consist of two sentences weakly linked together.

You can strengthen weak sentences in six main ways:
- Cutting up a long sentence into separate sentences
- Separating multiple sentences
- Cutting down long sentences
- Rebuilding a complicated sentence
- Making non-sentences whole
- Finding strong subjects and main verbs.

Some of these editing techniques require an understanding of grammar. These points will appear as the need arises.

Cutting up a long sentence into separate sentences

A sentence containing one idea is a *simple sentence*. A *compound sentence* consists of two simple sentences joined together. Cutting them apart may instantly create two stronger, simple sentences.

Conjunctions join simple sentences together into compound sentences. Look for the conjunctions and replace them, where possible, with a full stop and a capital letter. Sometimes the second sentence may need slight rewriting.

Conjunctions: *examples*

Conjunctions join words, ideas or sentences together. The most common are:
and, or, but, neither, before, after, until, when, although, as, since, so, so that, because, than, that, though, till, if, in order to, unless, nor, whereas, while, whilst, provided that, yet.

In all the following examples, the conjunction is marked in **bold**. Rewritten versions remove the conjunction; minor rewriting improves readability.

*I am under strict orders to collect all outstanding payments, **and** under the terms of our contract we have the authority to stop your credit facility.*
I am under strict orders to collect all outstanding payments. Under the terms of our contract, we have the authority to stop your credit facility.

*There is no space on the G:drive to open a file, **so** we have had to temporarily suspend any file creations.*
There is no space on the G:drive to open a file. We have, therefore, temporarily suspended any file creations.

*I expect the number of account transactions to increase during the second half of the year **as** most of the trading accounts were opened early in the year **and** it takes some time to educate the customer on the use of his account.*
I expect the number of account transactions to increase during the second half of the year. Most of the trading accounts were opened early in the year; it takes some time for customers to learn how to use their accounts.

*The action plan is likely to form the basis for future funding bids **and** it will be vital, therefore, to ensure that it is implementable **and** that it delivers the objectives of the operational themes in as cost-effective a manner as possible.*
The action plan is likely to form the basis for future funding bids. We must ensure, therefore, that it is practical, and that it meets operational objectives as cost-effectively as possible.

Separating multiple sentences

'Multiple sentences' are sentences joined together without a conjunction. You must separate these into individual sentences or use a conjunction.

Writers sometimes use 'however', 'therefore', or 'otherwise' to join sentences. These words are *adverbs*, not conjunctions. They cannot join sentences together. The simplest solution is to start a new sentence with the connecting word and follow it with a comma.

Below are some examples of 'multiple sentences' with suggested rewritten versions. The last example is a 'multiple sentence' including conjunctions.

I believe that you will be operating this system, if this is not the case please let me know.
I believe that you will be operating this system. If this is not the case, please let me know.

Due to unforeseeable circumstances, we will be unable to run this event on 20 October, however, we have made a provisional booking for the event on 4 November, please could you let me know if this is now inconvenient for you.

Due to unforeseen circumstances, we will be unable to run this event on 20 October. However, we have made a provisional booking for the event on 4 November. Please let me know if this is inconvenient for you.

Overall, the processes have been shown to be under control, however, specifications have been set on limited data and the control criteria and standard values do not appear to be appropriate and will now need to be reviewed.

Overall, the processes have been shown to be under control. However, specifications have been set on limited data. The control criteria and standard values do not appear to be appropriate. They must now be reviewed.

Cutting down a long sentence

Some sentences consist of a main idea and extra ideas that, themselves, could not be sentences. You may be able to cut down the length of the sentence by cutting out the extra idea, and, if necessary, presenting it elsewhere.

The extra idea may be a *subordinate clause* (an idea containing a finite verb). A sentence containing one or more subordinate clauses is called a *complex sentence*. Subordinate clauses are almost always surrounded by commas.

The example below includes a subordinate clause (in **bold**). You can reconstruct it as a complete sentence.

You may wish to raise an issue but not make a recommendation where you consider that, **whilst the matter does not yet constitute an unacceptable level or risk**, *it should still be brought to Management's attention.*

You may wish to bring an issue to Management's attention although it does not yet constitute an unacceptable level of risk. Where this is the case, you could raise the issue without making a recommendation.

The following example uses *that* and *which* to create an unwieldy sentence. Splitting the sentence at these words helps to make it easier to understand.

A daily transaction report is produced **that** *shows all the transactions posted to claims files,* **which** *is given back to the claims staff so they can check their own work.*

We produce a transaction report daily. This shows all the transactions posted to claims files. Claims staff receive this report so that they can check their own work.

Extra ideas in sentences are sometimes *prepositional phrases*: a group of words beginning with a preposition. Prepositional phrases, unlike subordinate clauses, do not normally take commas. Spot the preposition and you are on the way to finding ideas that you can move or remove.

Prepositions: *examples*

Prepositions precede nouns or pronouns. Here are the most common:

above, after, across, against, along, among, around, at, before, below, beneath, beside, between, beyond, by, down, during, for, from, in, near, of, off, on, over, since, through, to, under, underneath, until, up, with, without.

Beware! Some of these words can also function as adverbs (which usually qualify verbs). 'To' also commonly forms part of a verb: *to read, to walk, to manage* and so on. If the word comes before a noun, it is probably acting as a preposition.

In the following examples, the prepositions are in **bold** and the new versions remove as many as possible.

The purpose **of** *the headings is to enable the reader to scan the report very quickly,* **with** *a view* **to** *getting an overview* **of** *the issues which are being raised.*

The headings enable the reader to scan the report very quickly, so that they can see the issues which are being raised.

*The continued involvement **of** Rockshire Borough Council **in** the project is essential **to** the satisfactory continuation **of** the project to develop new services **for** elderly people **in** rural areas **of** the county.*
*Rockshire Borough Council must continue to be involved if the project is to continue developing new services for elderly people **in** the county's rural areas.*

*This approach, if implemented correctly, will allow the company to invest capital more efficiently or better utilize capital already set aside **by** allocating larger amounts **of** capital **to** high risk business segments and smaller amounts **to** lower risk business segments.*
This approach, if implemented correctly, will allow the company to invest capital more efficiently or better utilize capital already set aside. We will be able to allocate more capital to high risk business segments and less to lower risk business segments.

Rebuilding a complicated sentence

Sentences sometimes contain too many ideas knotted together. You can tell when this is happening because:
- the meaning is unclear
- the sentence contains too many words (over 25)
- there are very few verbs
- the verbs are feeble.

Unravel the ideas and reconstruct them, probably as a number of sentences. Don't be afraid to use more words than the original. No individual sentence should exceed 25 words.

Rebuilding a complicated sentence involves four steps:
1. Identify the **ideas** in the sentence. List them and ensure that they are in a logical order.
2. Rewrite each idea as a **separate sentence**. At this stage, discard the original version and work only with your new version.
3. Connect the sentences into **continuous prose**. Use link words or phrases to make the connections clearer.
4. Check your new version for **accuracy**, **brevity** and **clarity**. Cut down any lengthy expressions and replace long words with shorter ones.

Rebuilding a complicated sentence: *examples*

The costs to be taken into account are the costs of mains, sewers, treatment works and other capital works, including costs directly incurred by water or sewerage companies in developing supply sources in environmentally sensitive ways and in minimising the pollution caused by waste water disposal.

This sentence needs rebuilding.
- The meaning is unclear.
- The sentence is too long (46 words).
- There is only one main verb: *are*. The sentence contains an infinitive – to be – and a lot of words that look like verbs but aren't: *taken, including, incurred, developing, minimising* and *caused* are participles. This mass of participles in itself suggests that rebuilding is needed.
- The verb is feeble. The word *are*, from the verb *to be*, does little to show what is happening in the sentence.

1. Identify the **ideas** in the sentence. List them and ensure that they are in the correct logical order.
- *Costs to be taken into account*
- *Costs of mains, sewers, treatment works and other capital works*
- *Other capital works*
  a) developing supply sources in environmentally sensitive ways
  b) minimising pollution caused by waste water disposal.

2. Rewrite each idea as a separate sentence. At this stage, forget the original version entirely and work with your new version.
- *A number of costs need to be taken into account*
- *These include the costs of mains, sewers, treatment works and other capital works*
- *Capital works include*
-   *a) developing supply sources in environmentally sensitive ways*
-   *b) minimising the pollution caused by waste water disposal.*

Rebuilding a complicated sentence: *examples — continued*

3. Connect the sentences into continuous prose. Use link words or phrases to make the connections clearer.
A number of costs need to be taken into account. These include the costs of mains, sewers, treatment works and other capital works. Capital works include
a) developing supply sources in environmentally sensitive ways
b) minimising the pollution caused by waste water disposal.

4. Check your new version for accuracy, brevity and clarity. Cut down any lengthy expressions and replace long words with shorter ones.
We must take a number of capital costs into account. These include the costs of mains, sewers, treatment and other investment, such as
a) developing supply sources in environmentally sensitive ways
b) minimising pollution caused by waste water disposal.

Making non-sentences whole

Non-sentences are a very common mistake. The most common element missing is a verb – a 'doing' word that also places the sentence in time. Non-sentences can arise when you write a colloquial expression exactly as you would speak it.

These examples include some of the most common types of non-sentence, with some suggested alternatives:

Further to your letter of 1 May regarding overpayment of supply invoices.
Thank you for your letter about overpayment of supply invoices.

With reference to our telephone conversation on Friday.
We spoke on the phone last Friday./Thank you for calling us on Friday.

Due to a rise in the price of coffee from the suppliers.
Our suppliers have raised the price of coffee.

We have not been able to reconnect the power supply. The reason being that a major fault was discovered in the switching mechanism.
We have not been able to reconnect the power supply because we have discovered a major fault in the switching mechanism.

I am attaching a copy of our Request Document. If you could fill out a copy of this form for each consignment.
I attach a copy of our Request Document. Please fill out a copy of this form for each consignment.

Finding strong subjects and verbs

At the heart of a sentence is a relationship between a *subject* and a *verb*. The subject is the thing or person that the sentence is about. The verb expresses what the subject is doing or being. The subject and verb should be as strong and specific as possible. The strongest position for the subject and verb is at the start of the sentence. If the subject and verb are not at the beginning, try putting them there to improve the sentence's clarity.

This example swaps subjects around:

A particular strength has been the project structure.
The project structure has been particularly strong.

In this example, the subject and verb have moved to the front of the sentence:
At the heart of this new strategy is a focus on European growth.
A focus on European growth is at the heart of this new strategy.

The weakest subject is an *empty subject*. The word 'it' or 'there', as the subject of a sentence, contains no meaning; the reader must read the rest of the sentence to understand what it refers to.

In these examples, the empty subject is replaced with a more meaningful one:

It was stated that customer satisfaction was a high priority.
James stated that customer satisfaction was a high priority.

It is suggested that the policy should be consistent with budget constraints.
Policy should be consistent with budget constraints.

It is apparent that demand is now beginning to outstrip supply.
Demand is now outstripping supply.

In being clear, precise and unambiguous, it is often necessary to use technical terms and abbreviations.

It is good practice to explain each term on the first occasion it appears in the report.

To be clear, precise and unambiguous, technical terms and abbreviations may be necessary. Explain each term on the first occasion it appears in the report.

There is a risk that incorrect entries may be recorded on the system.

Incorrect entries may be recorded on the system. / Operators may record incorrect entries on the system.

There are two areas where controls are weak.

Controls are weak in two areas.

There is no evidence that customers are dissatisfied.

We have no evidence that customers are dissatisfied. / Customers do not seem to be dissatisfied.

There is a function on the software to ensure that passwords expire after a set period.

The software contains a function to ensure that passwords expire after a set period.

Editing words

English has a huge vocabulary: over 600,000 words, compared with 150,000 in French. One of the main reasons is that English often includes at least two words meaning roughly the same thing. We might *try, attempt* or *endeavour*; we could *start, begin, initiate* or *commence*; we might *help, aid, assist, enable, facilitate* or even *succour*. The choice of word depends on the context: how well you know your reader, what words you've used elsewhere, whether you are speaking a common professional language.

Shorter words are easier to understand than longer words. Of course, long words have their place. Sometimes a technical or unusual word will express exactly what you want to say. Technical language is plain to technical readers in the same field. You may need to explain the terms you use, either as you use them or in a glossary. Many long words, though, aren't specialized or technical; you can usually replace them with a short word that will do the job just as well.

The long and the short of it: *examples*

English is full of pairs of words with similar meanings: one long, one short. This list contains a few of the more common. Get into the habit of spotting these pairs of words, so that you can choose which to use. As a general rule, prefer the short word.

accordingly	so
acknowledge	thank
acquaint	tell
acquire	get, buy
additional	more
alleviate	lessen, reduce
ascertain	find out
assist	help
commence	start, begin
communicate	write, speak, tell
concept	idea
concerning	about
consequently	so
despatch	send
discontinued	ended, finished
endeavour	try
erroneous	wrong
establish	set up, create
expenditure	spending
facilitate	help
implement (verb)	carry out, do
initiate	start, begin
investigate	look into
proceed	go
purchase	buy
regarding	about
remittance	payment
request	ask
require	need
sufficient	enough
supplementary	extra, more
terminate	end
utilize	use

The commonest barriers to understanding at the word level are:

- passive verbs
- abstract nouns
- unnecessary words.

Passive verbs

Verbs can be either active or passive. An active verb expresses what its subject does; a passive verb expresses what its subject suffers, or has done to it. Sentences with active verbs are shorter, stronger and more dynamic than those with passive verbs.

Passive verbs are common in business writing: particularly reports, minutes and procedures. You may wish to use them if you don't know who did something (or if you don't want to admit who was responsible). Passive verbs can provide a more diplomatic tone. Too many passive verbs, though, will make your writing dull and lifeless.

Spotting a passive verb

A verb is *active* when its subject performs the action.
The meeting **agreed** *a plan of action.*
The manager **made** *a decision.*
The customer **has complained** *about the company's policy.*
A verb is *passive* when its subject suffers the action.
A plan of action **was agreed** *by the meeting.*
A decision **was made** *by the manager.*
A complaint **has been made** *by the customer about the company's policy.*
Passive verbs are always constructed from a finite part of the verb *to be* and a past participle (ending in *-ed, -en, -t,* or irregularly).

Convert passive verbs into the active by asking: 'Who or what is doing the action?' Put the 'operator' at the beginning of the sentence. Now ask: 'What is the verb?' Place the verb directly after the new subject and construct the rest of the sentence.

Here is a typical example from an operating procedure. All passive verbs are in **bold**.

Before setting up an agreement, we **must have been sent** *a letter from the customer confirming that the account* **is managed** *by the customer. This letter* **should be signed** *by one of the authorized signatories. The list of signatories* **can be obtained** *from Membership. Once a letter* **has been received** *by us, an agreement* **can be set up** *and the first exchange* **will be initiated**.

Make passive verbs active by placing the 'operator' in each case at the beginning of the clause. The result is clearer, crisper and easier to read.

Before setting up an agreement, we must receive a letter from the customer confirming that they manage the account. One of the authorized signatories should sign the letter. Membership hold the list of signatories. Once we have received a letter, we can set up an agreement and initiate the first exchange.

Report writers sometimes use passive verbs because they feel that a report must be objective. This example shows the kind of text that results.

Sound decisions **will be assisted** *by a clear statement of the objectives* **to be achieved** *by procedure x. Three possible objectives* **are discussed** *more fully below. However, it* **is to be noted** *that procedure x* **may not be considered** *the only means by which these objectives* **can be achieved**.

Begin by asking who is doing the actions in each case.

A clear statement of the objectives that we **intend to achieve** *will help us to make sound decisions about whether to use procedure x. The report discusses three possible objectives. However, we may not consider that procedure x is the only means by which we can achieve these objectives.*

Careful editing can remove some of the use of 'we' and tighten the writing still further.

Stating our objectives clearly will help us decide whether to use procedure x. The report discusses three possible objectives. However, procedure x may not be the only way of achieving them.

Minutes of meetings often contain many unnecessary passive verbs. This example is typical.

Concern **was expressed** *by some people about the format of our team meetings. It* **was acknowledged** *that information* **must be shared** *but*

it **was recognized** *that not everything* **can be known** *by all the team.*
It **was agreed** *also that not all decisions* **can be made** *unanimously.*
A rewrite eliminates 'minutespeak' and creates a crisper, shorter note.
Some people expressed concern about the format of our meetings. Of course
we must share information, but the whole team cannot know everything. We
agreed also that not all decisions can be unanimous.

Abstract nouns

Nouns name things, people, times, places or qualities. Concrete
nouns name things that are physically present in the world: *table,*
woman, pen, car, tree, window, machine, fire. Abstract nouns name things
that don't exist physically: *value, implementation, use, awareness, train-*
ing, growth, marketing, possibility.

Recognizing abstract nouns

An abstract noun names anything that doesn't physically exist: a
concept, idea, action or quality. The longest words we use are
often abstract nouns. They usually derive from verbs or
adjectives. You can sometimes identify them by their endings.

-tion	*(examination)*	*(examine)*
-ment	*(establishment)*	*(establish)*
-ance	*(performance)*	*(perform)*
-ence	*(reference)*	*(refer)*
-ure	*(expenditure)*	*(Expend/spend)*
-al	*(refusal)*	*(refuse)*
-age	*(leakage)*	*(leak)*
-ity	*(authority)*	*(authorize)*
	(equality)	*(equal)*
	(responsibility)	*(responsible)*

Gerunds are participles of verbs used as abstract nouns. They
always end in *-ing.*

acting	*raising*	*budgeting*
deciding	*implementing*	*communicating*
walking	*working*	*writing*

Concrete nouns work in part by creating pictures in the reader's mind. Abstract nouns don't stimulate the imagination nearly so easily. They create fog in the reader's mind rather than images.

Business English tends to use a lot of abstract nouns. Remove them wherever you can. You may be able to use a verb or adjective, or substitute a more concrete noun ('train' for 'rail transport', for example).

In these examples, abstract nouns (in **bold**) become verbs or adjectives.

*The **usage** of the system has increased significantly since May.*
Managers have used the system significantly more since May.

*There has been an **expansion** in our asset management activity over the past year.*
Our asset management has expanded over the past year.

*The **majority** of users clear their in-trays within 48 hours.*
Most users clear their in-trays within 48 hours.

*The **proposal** is to file all e-mails electronically.*
We propose to file all e-mails electronically.

***Payment** can be made by cheque or cash.*
You can pay by cheque or cash.

*The use of these strategies requires the **commitment** of staff **resources** (for example, in preparing **guidance**). However, improved **confidence** exists that this **procedure** will yield greater data **reliability**, **completeness** and **consistency**.*
If we use these strategies, we must commit staff (for example, to help guide the committee). However, we are confident that this approach will give us data that are more reliable, complete and consistent.

Abstract nouns often appear in clusters: a string of nouns that create an almost impenetrable description of a process or idea. You may be able to manage a cluster of two words: 'management development', for example, or 'communication skills'. But how about this?
***Inadequacies** in the **provision** of staff **performance review opportunities** during the year have occurred.*
We have had too few opportunities this year to review staff performance.

Unnecessary words

Some words contribute nothing to meaning. You might use them because they sound good, or because you don't quite know what to say next. If you write the first draft in your own voice, you will almost certainly put in some redundant words and phrases. Take them out at the editing stage, leaving only the words that are necessary to your meaning.

Redundant words: *examples*

Redundant words don't do any work: they add no further meaning. Here are some of the most common.

in the event that	in anticipation of
with reference to	with regard to
each and every	first and foremost
for all intents and purposes	generally speaking
and so on	final outcome
right and proper	initial preparation
the reason for	due to the fact that

These examples dispense with unnecessary words.

I would be grateful if you could reply to this letter.
Please reply to this letter.

Can you advise me of your product requirements.
Please tell me what products you need.

Please let us know your intentions in writing as to whether you wish to continue in membership.
Please let me know in writing whether you wish to remain in membership.

Thank you for writing to us in the matter of your accommodation requirements. At this point in time, we are not in a position to offer you anything suitable owing to the fact that no flats answering to the description you have forwarded to us are presently lodged on our books.
Thank you for telling us the kind of flat you are looking for. At present, we cannot offer you anything suitable because we have no flats available that meet your needs.

Since I am unsure of the importance of this clause, I would be most grateful if you could advise me as to the implications of the above being omitted so that I may make a judgement as to whether we should have it put in.
I am unsure how important this clause is. Please let me know the conse quences of leaving it out, so that I can decide whether to include it.

CHAPTER 7

Bringing your writing to life

At a glance

Good writing comes alive in the reader's mind. Style is personal and bringing your writing to life is a long-term project.
- Say what you mean.
- Be specific.
- Be positive.
- Remove blockages.
- Read around.

Effective writing comes alive in your mind. As you read, you sense the writer speaking to you directly. Nothing comes between the writer's meaning and your understanding. Effective writing is transparently clear.

Bringing your own writing alive is a long-term project. It is a matter of experience and taste: you can improve your style only by practising regularly and developing a discriminating eye. Here are some guidelines to point you in the right direction.
- Say what you mean.
- Be specific.
- Be positive.
- Remove blockages.
- Read around.

Style is personal. Choosing how to write is like choosing how to dress. We wear different clothes in different situations; similarly, we write differently according to the circumstances. At work, we dress to give the impression of professionalism; our writing should do the same.

Improving your style is like developing your dress sense. You might choose clothes by looking at what others wear, asking friends for their opinions and keeping an eye on fashion in the outside world. In just the same way, you can develop your writing style by reading what others write, asking for second thoughts on documents you've produced and reading around.

Say what you mean

Concentrate on what you want to say, not on the way you say it. Imagine the reader's response. If you had only a few seconds to get the point across, what would you say?

What are your key messages?

Write them down as boldly as possible. Work out the best places for them: at the beginning of the document/section/paragraph.

Imagine speaking what you've written

How does it sound? How might it sound to the reader? How could you say what you want to say more simply? Speak aloud and write *exactly* what you say (you might consider using a tape recorder).

Be sincere

Don't wrap up your meaning in polite language. Good manners become exaggerated on paper: your reader may even think you're hiding something. Resist feeling that you must soften the blow of a negative or awkward message with friendly words. The reader may interpret your tone as shifty, evasive, dishonest. If you feel that your message may provoke an unwelcome response in the reader, change the message. What response do you want? What could you say to them to achieve it?

Don't use scaffolding

Avoid describing what you have been doing, are doing or will do in the document.
I am writing to . . .
The aim of this letter is to . . .

We have been discussing . . .
So far, I've covered . . .
In this part of the report, I will . . .
Before we go on to . . . we must try to understand . . .
I turn now to . . .
I have done my best to explain why . . .

Be specific

Aim to be precise rather than vague. Say exactly what you mean rather than generalizing. Avoid sweeping statements that you may not be able to support.

Use numbers

Numbers will make your point more specific. It's important to ration them, so that the reader isn't blinded by statistics. What is the most significant number? What statistic best supports your point?

Words and phrases with a general sense of amount or number are usually value-loaded. Avoid these:

several, numerous, extensive, excessively, insufficient, massive, enormous, big, long, small, tiny, undersized, minimal, a significant increase, an unacceptable number of, to a considerable extent.

Give your reader measured amounts and quantities to justify any judgement.

Write personally

Professionalism means relating personally to colleagues and customers. Much business writing struggles to come to life because writers feel they must remove themselves from it. Perhaps they've been told that business or technical writing must be objective, impersonal or in the third person.

Writing personally means allocating responsibility wherever possible. Who (or what) did what? Name them. The reader will then have a much stronger picture of what happened.

Use personal pronouns wherever appropriate:

I, you, he, she, it, we, you, they.

'You' is more lively than 'the customer'; 'we' has more life than 'the company'. Make sure that your reader can see who or what the pronoun refers to. For example, who is 'we'? Do you mean 'you' (the reader) and 'I' (the writer)? 'I' and a colleague? The team? The department? The company? The profession? The general public?

Take care, too, not to use any one pronoun too much. 'You' can sound accusing in the wrong context; 'I' can seem self-centred if over-used.

Use verbs with a specific meaning

Avoid verbs that don't mean much, or whose meaning is generalized:

get, make, carry out, perform, give, conduct, implement, move, do.

It's easy to over-use the verbs *to be* or *to have*. Find crisper, clearer alternatives.

Make it concrete

Concrete nouns appeal to the senses and stimulate the reader's imagination. If you express an idea or concept in one sentence, bring it to life by using specific, concrete examples in the next.

Use jargon carefully

The word *jargon* has always suggested nonsense or gibberish. It originally meant the chattering of birds, and hence came to mean any unintelligible babble. Only later did it come to refer to the specialized language of a profession, skill or group.

Jargon has its place. Specialized terms are a kind of shorthand that allow us to express complicated ideas quickly. The same is true of buzzwords, in-house language and abbreviations. If your reader understands the exact meaning of a specialized word, use it. If in doubt, find another word. Often, of course, people lose sight of jargon's exact meaning and use it lazily, or as a membership badge. Then jargon reverts to gibberish.

If necessary, you can introduce your reader to jargon in the document. You might use a glossary, listing the terms alphabetically with short sentence definitions. Place the glossary at the end or near the start of a document, or perhaps on a foldout so that the reader can use it more easily. In shorter, less technical documents, you could define terms as you introduce them, emphasizing the term itself and placing the definition in brackets immediately after.

All codes should be **compliant** *(formatted for use in all parts of the internal network).*

The same applies to names: explain what it refers to immediately after you introduce the name.

Staff should understand the workings of tools such as COMPARE (which compares outputs from different parts of the network).

Abbreviations are usually introduced differently: the abbreviation in brackets after the full expression of the name or term.

Minimal volume was delivered Over-The-Counter (OTC).

Most computer information is delivered through the Integrated Services Digital Network (ISDN).

This technique only works well in short documents. In longer documents, gather definitions into a glossary.

Be positive

Be forward-looking and action-centred. Avoid writing too much about what has happened, what hasn't happened, what should have happened, what's wrong.

The Service Department has regularly failed to deliver monthly worksheets.

We cannot deliver the goods before 15 September.

Monitoring procedures are inadequate.

Write about what is happening, what will happen, what should happen, how to put things right, what you are doing.

The Service Department is now committed to delivering monthly worksheets.

We will deliver the goods on 15 September.

We need to improve monitoring procedures.

Make definite promises – and make sure that you can keep them.
I will do my best to hold the tickets for you.
I will hold the tickets in your name for three days.

Generate in the reader the feeling appropriate to your message. Emotive language clouds the issue and hides the message. On paper, a momentary outburst is permanently recorded and can return to haunt us.
Your failure to reply . . .
Your refusal to cooperate . . .
It surprises me that someone of your undoubted intelligence should have misunderstood my letter so utterly and completely.

Use language that is sincere and definite.
I have not yet received a reply . . .
As you feel that we should no longer work together . . .
I would be happy to clarify anything that remains unclear.

Remove blockages

Good writing flows, like water in a pipe. The language is under pressure, and nothing blocks the flow of meaning. Bring your writing to life by removing the blockages, clearing whatever gets in the way of your meaning.

We have already seen in Chapter 6 how removing passive verbs, abstract nouns and redundant words can improve the flow. Further obstructions include:

- clichés
- pompous language
- unvarying sentence construction.

Destroy clichés

A cliché was originally a block of type containing the whole of a common phrase; printers used them to save time when setting up a page of print. The word has come to mean a hackneyed phrase that blocks the flow of meaning around it.

Clichés for our time: *examples*

Clichés, as they say, come and go. Many are metaphors, expressing an abstract idea in concrete terms. Be on the lookout for the latest cliché on the block and resist putting it in the frame.

take on board
the bottom line
outside the box
put on hold
suck it and see
a whole new ball game
come out of the closet
conventional wisdom
when it comes to the crunch
as such
the nitty-gritty

at the end of the day
a quantum leap
a key player
state of the art
up and running
at the cutting edge
put on the back burner
fundamentally flawed
at this point in time
when push comes to shove
a cast iron copper-bottomed guarantee

Deflate pompous language

Some writers think that using long or unusual words makes them look more dignified, businesslike or important. The effect is more likely to be the opposite: the reader may well think them pompous, officious and self-important.

There are no absolute rules here. A word may look inflated to one reader and normal to another. As a broad guideline, choose shorter simpler words wherever you can.

Deflating pomposity: *examples*

You can easily tell if a word is inflated. If you removed it, would you need a long phrase to say the same thing? If so, you probably need the word. If not, find a single shorter or more ordinary word, and use that.

Thousands of pompous words need deflating. Here are a few, with suggested alternatives.

Deflating pomposity: *examples – continued*

aggregation	total
approximately	about
ascertain	find out
cognisant of	aware of, knowing
commendation	praise
customary channels	usual way
educational institution	school, college, university
effect	make, do
envisage	see, foresee
facilitate	help
functionality	what it can do
grant dispensation	allow
implement	do
instrumentality	means, ways
subseqent to	after

Vary your sentence construction

Sentences come in three main types: simple, compound and complex. Appendix B summarizes the grammar of sentence construction.

Using one kind of sentence too much creates a blockage in readers' minds by exhausting them. The most common problem is probably over-use of complex sentences, in which subordinate ideas are added to main ideas. (The previous sentence is complex. The two sentences in these brackets are simple.) Too many complex sentences make your writing indigestible. Too many simple sentences, on the other hand, will create a disjointed effect.

Create a rich mix of simple, compound and complex sentences. Use simple sentences for your biggest ideas. Place them prominently, at the beginnings and ends of paragraphs or sections. Try not to put too many complex sentences together. Cut down on prepositions.

Read around

Good writers feed on other writing. They devour print whenever they can, stealing ideas from colleagues, scanning marketing literature and browsing in the company library. Above all, they read outside the organization. Everything is grist to the mill: magazines, books, letters in the newspaper, the back of the cereal packet.

Read whatever interests you. Try to read something new every day. Your taste for good writing will develop, almost without your noticing it; that critical sense will pass into your own work.

CHAPTER 8

Effective layout

At a glance

Good writing needs good layout. The key principles of layout are legibility and attractiveness; the three variables that make most difference are:
- font or typeface
- space on the page
- highlighting techniques.

Fonts are broadly categorized as serif or sanserif. For large areas of text, serif is probably best. Sanserif fonts are seen as modern, cosmopolitan and user-friendly. Mixing the two kinds of font can be effective, particularly using sanserif for headings and serif for text.

Don't fill the page with too much text. Be generous with margins and consider making the right-hand margin ragged rather than justified. Create space between paragraphs and lines, and under headings.

Emphasize simply and sparingly. Use bold to emphasize definition and italics to distinguish tone. Avoid capital letters and underlining. Use colour sparingly.

Good writing needs good layout. Until recently, writers could control only a few elements of visual or graphic display. Wordprocessing software and DTP packages now offer a bewilderingly wide range of graphic techniques. Used well – which almost always means used sparingly – they can add to the impact and quality of your documents.

Many elements of layout may be prescribed for you in a style guide or company regulations. This chapter will help you in those areas where you can choose how your text looks.

The key principles of good layout are:
- legibility
- attractiveness.

Text is legible if the reader can recognize individual letters easily and quickly. It's attractive if readers are likely to want to pick up the page and read it.

The three variables that contribute most to effective layout are:
- font or typeface
- space on the page
- highlighting techniques.

In this chapter, I'm assuming that you are using A4 paper (210 × 297 mm). This is the most common paper size in use today. I'm also assuming that you don't want to put your text into columns, grids or boxes. If you are considering different paper sizes or layout designs – for reports, leaflets, newsletters or fliers giving public information – you need to investigate desk-top publishing and design.

Font or typeface

Fonts are broadly categorized as serif or sanserif. Serifs – the tiny hooks, feet and brackets on the letters – make serif fonts generally more readable.

This is a serif typeface.

This is a sanserif typeface.

For large areas of text, a serif font is probably best. The letters' serifs guide the eye along the page, and their variations in thickness give the page irregular patterns of light and shade. Serif fonts have an elegant, classical, authoritative look.

Sanserif typefaces are generally seen as modern, cosmopolitan and user-friendly. They deliver small amounts of information very effectively. They are particularly suitable for headings, titles and summaries. They work well in forms, catalogues, promotional material, fliers and notices.

In large areas of text, a sanserif font gives the page a friendly, unfussy, unofficial look. It can make the text feel less serious; you may consider this an advantage. I feel that it can also give a somewhat 'temporary' look to the text. There is some evidence, too, that people don't read sanserif as carefully as a serif font.

Mixing serif and sanserif can be especially effective if done carefully and unfussily. Using sanserif for headings and serif for text is common and works well. Try reversing the convention and see what effect you create. Of course, both serif and sanserif fonts come in *italic* versions.

Broadly, then, you have four options in choosing fonts: serif and sanserif, and italic in each. Use them consistently. Establish some basic conventions and stick to them. The worst error is to go wild and use too many different fonts in one piece of text. Two fonts will suffice for most situations.

A further important factor is point size: the size of the letters on the page. For a page of A4 text, 9-point and above is usually considered readable. Different fonts will create different effects, even at the same point size, because of the relative proportions of the letter designs. A point size somewhere between 12 and 15 is probably about right.

The font that you use should be quiet, simple and regular. You should use it consistently across documents of similar types. What works well for a letter, however, may not be suitable for a report or a set of instructions.

Space on the page

The most common problem in page layout is that the writer fills the page with too much text. If in doubt, use too much space rather than too little. Consider the overall impression of the page: its visual balance and attractiveness. Use a second page rather than cramming everything onto one side.

Margins

Be generous with your margins. Narrow margins somehow suggest that you are more interested in saving paper than in communicating clearly.

Adjust point size and margin width to create a column of between 50 and 70 character spaces, or about 12 words per line.

A *scholar's margin* can be useful in reports, instructions and technical documents. This is a wide margin – about 70 mm – usually on the left of the page. It creates space for readers to make notes and is especially useful to lighten dense text or technical detail.

Justification

Justification means lining up the text to create straight vertical edges. Left margins are almost always justified: a ragged left edge creates text that's much harder to read.

The case for right justification is not so clear-cut. Certainly, it uses space more economically. Most publishers probably continue to use it in books for this reason (although some now use an unjustified right margin to help give the book a more 'luxurious' image). Right justification gives the page a very official appearance, particularly in letters. More seriously, it can contribute to 'vertical pull', dragging the eye down the page rather than along the lines of text. It can be especially unpleasant in conjunction with a small typeface, or if the computer has to pull words apart to adjust line length. Hyphenation may compensate for this effect; the price may be a lot of words broken in the middle.

An unjustified right margin creates a more inviting layout. It is more personal, relaxed and informal – and seems to make for easier reading. Research suggests that it can increase comprehension by 55%. A ragged right edge will also cancel the need for hyphenation. Any letter will benefit from a ragged right margin; many a report will look better for it.

Space within the text

Creating space within the text is as important as putting space around it. The horizontal areas of space between paragraphs, headings and lines of text contribute a lot to legibility and attractiveness.

Put two carriage returns between paragraphs. Avoid carrying the last line of a paragraph over a page break, and remember also that a paragraph break occurring exactly on the page turn may not register with the reader.

Ensure that headings have more space above than below. They should clearly relate to the section following them. Use indenting to create space around sub-paragraphs or bullet points. If your right margin is ragged, don't indent too much.

Two elements of white space are often overlooked. The space between the lines – sometimes called 'leading' – should be about a fifth of the point size. The space between letters can be adjusted by 'tracking' or 'scaling'. There are no hard rules about this: be sensitive to the look of the text on the page and make sure that the words look neither too stretched nor too cramped.

Highlighting techniques

Emphasize simply and sparingly. You will often want to emphasize elements in the text in the hope that the reader won't miss the point. The greatest danger is that you will overdo it. Emphasize too much and you will emphasize nothing.

You can create emphasis by varying:
- the weight of the typeface (usually called 'bold')
- point size (the size of the letters)
- the style of font (italic).

Other techniques include using capital letters and underlining. Increasingly, colour is becoming available.

Vary the weight of the text to emphasize **definition**. Bold text works well for headings and to highlight individual meanings within the text: specialized terms, important details in instructions. Use as few weights as you can and make them clearly distinguishable. Vary the weight of the font principally for headings. Within the text, use bold only for a very few words at a time. Set up a 'hierarchy of headings' with set weights and point sizes for each level of heading: chapter, section or letter heading, sub-heading and paragraph heading. Make sure you use the hierarchy consistently throughout the document to create signposts for the reader.

Use italics to create a distinction of *tone*. Italics help you to vary the 'tone of voice' in your writing.

Capital letters and underlining are best avoided. CAPITAL LETTERS LOOK AGGRESSIVE. They also decrease legibility.

Use a mixture of upper and lower case for headings. <u>Underlining looks increasingly old-fashioned as a method of emphasis</u>. It can also make the bottoms of the letters difficult to read, particularly those with vertical strokes below the line.

Colour printing has been available for some years. It can add variety and interest to the page, if used well. It can also give the material a 'quality' appearance, particularly in association with a better quality of paper. You could colour the text or shade an area – probably within a box. Keep the number of colours small. Use colours as navigation aids: to emphasize headings (or one level of heading), to indicate summary, action or recommendation boxes, and to give front covers added emphasis.

Different colours give different impressions. Blue is apparently the most popular colour in the UK; green is seen as restful, positive and informative; red obviously has connotations of urgency or danger. Once again, consistency and economy are important. Use the same colour for the same function. You may like to set up a 'colour code' in your documents so that readers become used to seeing the same parts of the document shaded in the same colour. Remember that some colours will not photocopy well into black and white. As a general rule, colour text strongly and shaded areas lightly.

CHAPTER 9

Memos and e-mails

At a glance

Memos and e-mails usually deliver simple messages within an organization. You should need to do little to turn an outline into a memo. Consider P-A-D (Purpose, Action, Deadline) boxes as an alternative format for heading the memo. Beware of writing memos as 'streams of consciousness' or 'long stories'. 'E-mail etiquette' brings its own problems. Make the message doubly clear. Minimize the supporting information. Don't 'shout' or write 'flames' (emotional outbursts). Avoid tricks. Edit carefully before sending. Remember that all e-mail is public and don't send 'spam' (junk e-mails). Clear your in-box regularly.

Memos and e-mails usually deliver simple messages within an organization. E-mails may travel outside the organization; on these occasions, think of them as electronic letters.

E-mail is developing its own conventions: 'e-mail etiquette'. To avoid confusion, the details of best practice in e-mail appear separately in this chapter.

You should need to do little to turn an outline into a finished memo. The briefest memo might only be one line long, delivering the message and nothing more. Problems begin to arise when the memo gets longer: do you need to input any supporting information? If so, how much, and in what order? Outlining should answer these questions without too much difficulty. Make sure that your message stays at the top, and that your paragraphs reflect the order and number of main points in the outline.

Heading the memo

Most memos are written on standard forms looking something like this:

Memorandum

> To:
> From:
> Date:
> Subject:

Many organizations are coming to see that this standard heading leaves much to be desired. The word 'Subject', especially, gives no clue to writer or reader of the memo's *purpose*, and can make for unfocused writing.

P-A-D Boxes

> P-A-D boxes provide a useful way of heading memos. The top of the page has three boxes for Purpose, Action and Deadline. The writer can place his/her statement of purpose – in brief form – in the first box, the action point in the second and the latest date for action in the third. $(P-A-D)$
>
> *PURPOSE*
> To identify sales figures required for quarterly report
>
> *ACTION*
> Please supply total product sales for European territories for January to March
>
> *DEADLINE*
> 12 April
>
> The reader can see immediately what the writer is asking them to do and sort the memos into priority order.

Putting memos right

Poor memos tend to fall into two categories:

- streams of consciousness
- long stories.

A 'stream of consciousness' memo records the *process* of the writer's thinking. Ideas appear in the order the writer thought them, with the conclusion – the most important point – at the end. If challenged, the writer might say: 'I want the reader to follow my thinking and come to the same conclusion.' Unfortunately, the reader rarely wants to follow the course of the writer's thinking; he needs to know the conclusion and any arguments or evidence to support it.

Make your point; then support it

A 'stream of consciousness' memo violates this golden rule. Find the conclusion and place it at the *beginning* as your message. Ask what the reader needs to know to understand the message in more detail and complete the memo with that supporting information.

Improving a 'stream of consciousness' memo: *example*

TO: Bob   FROM: Hilary   DATE: 30 April
RE: Finance meeting: Tuesday 3 pm
Jo Smith phoned this morning to say she can't make the meeting at 3pm on Tuesday. Sarah says she doesn't mind holding it later, or even on Wednesday, but not before 11 am. I've spoken to Mike's secretary: she says he now won't be back from Tokyo until Tuesday night anyway. It looks like it will have to be on Wednesday. I've checked with Sarah, and Mike's secretary, and they can make this, and Meeting Room 4 is free at 11 am on that day. Is this OK for you?

This is a typical 'stream of consciousness' memo: the message is in the last sentence. By placing it at the head of the memo, you can immediately see what information you might need to support it. The result is clearer, crisper and more action-centred.
Can we reschedule Tuesday's finance meeting for Wednesday at 11 am? This would allow Jo Smith, Sarah and Mike to attend. The venue is Meeting Room 4.

'Long story' memos record a sequence of events in the past. Stories are almost always of no interest to your reader because they aren't useful. A narrative structure cannot easily help them to make a decision. A story tells what happened in the past; your reader is more interested in what to do *now*.

Improving a 'long story' memo: *example*

TO: Liz   FROM: Lesley   DATE: 1 August
RE: Huckleborough visit: 31 July
I visited Huckleborough yesterday to assess the feasibility of taking on rented accommodation within a 5 mile radius of the TARA project.
I was met by Mike Woolbury of Beechcroft Estate Agents who discussed our requirements and showed me around. The old town in Huckleborough is very nice and incorporates some large properties that may be suitable for us. There are a lot of large housing estates on the outskirts, however, and a large number of major companies moving into the area and therefore in direct competition with us for rented accommodation. Parking seems a problem (lots of restrictions, not much off road parking that I could see). We viewed only two properties: Garrison Court, a small set of apartments, poorly furnished and equipped – not acceptable. And The Bourne, a cul-de-sac just completed and very close to a council estate – not really our style.
I think the best course of action might be for London-based staff to commute from their homes (Huckleborough is only 30 mins. out) and for staff from the north to be put up at the Castlehouse hotel on the ring road (modern hotel with swimming pool but no gym). Obviously this is only a suggestion but from my visit I feel that good accommodation is going to be hard to come by and it seems that the crime rate in the area is quite high.
I hope this is useful. When you have had a chance to review it please call me so we can discuss.

Extracting the relevant message from this memo is not easy – especially for the reader. The key to rewriting it is to ask what actions the writer is proposing.
The most obvious action point is asking the reader to phone the writer. You might rewrite:
Please call me to discuss accommodation arrangements for the TARA project.
– and leave it at that. Or you may decide that you want to brief the reader by identifying the two possible solutions to the

---

Improving a 'long story' memo: *example – continued*

problem that you can see. Your message then becomes:

I can see two solutions to the accommodation problem for the TARA project.

You then outline the two solutions, perhaps emphasizing them using numbers, indenting or bullet points. The final memo would then look like this:

I can see two solutions to the accommodation problem for the TARA project.

- *London-based staff can commute from their homes (Huckleborough is only 30 minutes out).*
- *Staff from the north can stay at the Castlehouse hotel on the ring road. This is a modern hotel with a swimming pool (but no gym).*

My visit on 31 July convinced me that good accommodation is hard to find in Huckleborough and that these options are the easiest and most cost-effective.

Please call me to discuss.

E-mail etiquette

E-mail is fast taking over from memos for sending internal messages. It's fast, cheap, paperless and – theoretically – efficient. It enables virtually instant communication from person to person, within a team or across the whole organization. Managers and staff can use e-mail to relieve the curse of constant interruptions, to keep in touch on the move and to prioritize workloads. E-mail spans time zones and distances at no extra cost and can help to break down bureaucratic barriers.

But e-mail also brings its own problems.

- *Information overload.* The biggest problem in writing an e-mail may be getting noticed. Just as new roads seem to generate more traffic, e-mail seems to generate more messages roaming the network. A recent survey suggested that managers receive an average of 178 e-mails a day. One manager I spoke to claimed to receive 500

e-mails daily. This intolerable situation is the result of:
- writers 'copying in' readers unnecessarily
- managers receiving e-mails simply because they have an e-mail address
- 'spam': electronic junk mail, either internal or from commercial sources.

People are beginning to develop coping strategies for dealing with the overload. They may delete an e-mail simply on the basis of who sent it. They may test a message's urgency by refusing to answer until it appears more than four or five times.

- *Death of the conversation.* In some organizations, people now hardly talk to each other at all; *all* communication is by e-mail. Decisions that should take minutes are unresolved for days. Managers use e-mail as an excuse for not being available. Lonely 'cubicle workers' try to use e-mail as a substitute for social contact: gossip clogs up the system. E-mail has taken on a style of its own: private jargon, cryptic symbols and a kind of ungrammatical, over-colloquial language that often confuses rather than clarifies.
- *More haste, less understanding.* Because of its speed, writers feel that e-mail needn't be carefully written. Too many writers send e-mails without checking even the spelling. Within the organization, messages become garbled; outside the organization, clients and partners get an impression of carelessness and laziness.
- *Overflowing in-boxes.* Undeleted e-mails are causing the electronic equivalent of paper mountains.

E-mails are written communication. Treat them with the same care as other kinds of writing. *All the guidelines that apply to memos apply equally to e-mails.*

Here are ten more tips to help e-mail work better for you.

1. Make the message clear

Nothing is more important than your message. Make sure that your e-mail makes a clear point, expressed in a single sentence of 15 words or less. Put it up front, on its own line, at the head of the text.

2. Minimize information

The less information you give, the more likely the reader will be to read it. Make a few points, displaying them with short paragraphs and bullet points. Restrict the material to the size of the screen. People are reluctant to scroll down to read more.

3. Put the message in the subject line

The subject line 'sells' your e-mail. Reading the subject line is the only way your reader can decide whether to read your message and how to prioritize messages.

Put your message – or an abbreviated version of it – into the subject line. Include a verb or some other sign of action.

4. Don't shout

In the network jungle, it can be difficult to get noticed. Writers resort to using capital letters, colour or cries of 'Urgent!' and 'Read this now!!'

Shouting, in whatever way, is usually counterproductive. In particular, MESSAGES WRITTEN ENTIRELY IN CAPITAL LETTERS ARE HARD TO READ AND CAN SEEM AGGRESSIVE – <u>EVEN MORE SO IF UNDERLINED</u>, **WRITTEN IN BOLD OR SUPPORTED WITH EXCESSIVE PUNCTUATION!!!!!**.

The best ways to get your reader's attention are:
– to send e-mails only when you have to
– to summarize your message in the subject line
– to use ★ stars ★ to emphasize small parts of the e-mail
– to gain a reputation for being succinct.

5. Don't fan 'flames'

'Flames' are personal insults or expressions of extreme feeling. They are usually impulsive reactions to stress, tiredness or annoyance. Flames are on the increase, perhaps because it's much easier to be nasty to someone on e-mail than face-to-face.

Stop, take a deep breath, and put out the fire. Flames can burn out your career.

6. Avoid e-mail trickery

E-mail has begun to generate stylistic tricks in an attempt to create a sense of conversation. The most common is to combine a kind of chatty shorthand with waffling gossip. Write in complete sentences and only include what is useful and productive.

Certain acronyms are becoming current on e-mail. Among them are:

- IMHO (in my humble opinion)
- BTW (by the way)
- FWIW (for what it's worth)
- LOL (laughing out loud).

None of these is necessary. Don't use them.

Some consultancies promote 'emoticons' to help you, in their words, 'convey expression' and 'ensure that your e-mail doesn't lose personality'. If you see ':-)', for example, you are supposed to understand that the writer is smiling – sideways. Perhaps they make for a playful diversion for a moment. But they also detract from the message. Express yourself clearly in words and your personality will shine through.

7. Edit before sending

Once you send a message, it's gone. Because it's instantaneous, e-mail earns you the time to check that you've got it right. You will be judged on the quality of your communication skills; a few moments checking details will make for a good impression at the other end.

Check that you've attached only the relevant files. Check that you are sending the message to the appropriate person, and that the address is correct. Is your 'cc' list too long? Send e-mails only to those who need to know – not to everyone you know.

Check your presentation. Review grammar, punctuation and spelling. How does your e-mail look? Neat and tidy – or fussy, over-designed and a riot of colour?

8. Remember that e-mail is public

Every e-mail leaves a trace. Don't assume that deleting an e-mail from your PC will destroy it. In most organizations, the message is stored more permanently on an internet server or network server computer.

E-mail is now admissible as evidence in courts of law and industrial tribunals. Obviously, sexist or racist messages are utterly unacceptable and may prove to be illegal. Think twice before sending anything confidential or commercially sensitive over the network.

Only send e-mails that you would be happy to show anybody – including a lawyer.

9. Don't 'spam'

'Spam' is jargon for electronic junk mail. 'To spam' is to intrude on others' mail with unwanted material. 'Spamming' is particularly common in news groups and user group forums. You know you've been 'spammed' when you receive a message you don't need. And, if you send an inappropriate or irrelevant message to anybody, I suppose you've become a 'spammer'.

Don't be tempted to broadcast an e-mail to an entire population. A 'cc' list of half a page is not a status symbol; it's a sign of operational ineffectiveness. Remember, too, that e-mail is a working tool. It's not the place for personal messages or opinions, nor for chat or gossip.

10. Clear your in-box regularly

Have you accumulated hundreds of messages in your in-box? You're taking up valuable space on the network. Set aside a few minutes each month to delete all outdated messages. You'll make both yourself and the network more efficient – and you'll feel better for it.

CHAPTER 10

Letters

At a glance

Every business letter should seek to develop a professional relationship and be action-centred.

Make sure the letter's message is at the top of your outline. Add an action point at the end of the letter and 'handshakes' at the start and end to frame it.

The best way to get the letter's tone right is to read it aloud.

Beware of being too formal. Be positive, definite and sincere.

Pay attention to the salutation, heading and the handshakes of the letter. Blocked layout is the most common modern layout.

Take care with the complimentary close, the signature line, references, date and any extra elements.

Letters develop relationships – between friends, colleagues, or total strangers. The nature of the relationship dictates the nature of the letter. An effective business letter is precise, straightforward and – above all – action-centred.

Every letter should be personal. Too many business letters look like the products of machines. Readers feel annoyed with letters that are obviously computer-generated. If you use standard paragraphs or letters, take great care. Personalize them as much as you can and review them regularly to stop them becoming stale.

Letters are an expensive way to communicate. A business letter can cost upwards of £20 to produce. A telephone call might clarify matters more quickly – and cheaply. Sending a fax or e-mail may be cheaper and more efficient. The time saved in sending the document by fax or e-mail gives you extra time for planning and editing. Regard faxes and e-mails as electronic letters; don't let the technology seduce you into sloppiness which could cause problems and delays later.

You may need to check that you have the authority to write the letter. If you are signing it, you are legally responsible for it, even when signing 'pp' on behalf of another – unless the signature is accompanied by the disclaimer: 'Dictated by . . . and signed in their absence.'

Creating a letter from an outline

Your outline includes the letter's message – the single most important thing you want to say to the reader – and the main points that support it. Take particular care to create a message that is acceptable to your reader: in terms they understand, in a tone that is appropriate. Check, too, that your main points are in a logical order. Put your action point *last*.

Note that your message, as always, is *at the top* of the outline. Don't be tempted to push it further down into the letter – especially if it is bad news.

The outline changes slightly to become the letter's first draft. The main adaptations are:
- an action point placed at the end of the letter, in its own paragraph
- 'handshakes' at the beginning and end.

The letter will also include all the usual apparatus of correspondence:
- reader's name and address
- reference numbers
- date
- salutation
- a heading
- complimentary close
- writer's name and job title
- 'cc' list of names copied to.

Business letter: *basic structure*

Salutation: *Dear Reader*
Heading
Opening 'handshake': establish relationship
Paragraph: message sentence
Paragraph: main point 1
Paragraph: main point 2
. . .
Paragraph: final main point
Paragraph: action point
Paragraph: closing 'handshake'
Complimentary close: *Yours sincerely/faithfully*
WRITER'S NAME
Writer's job title

Getting the tone right

The best way to check the letter's tone is to speak it aloud. When you speak, you naturally adapt your tone to your listener: their status, age, relationship to the organization, cultural background and so on. Write what you would say to your reader if you were talking to them. Correct for grammar if necessary, but try not to use any words or phrases that you wouldn't use when you speak. In particular, beware of being too formal. A letter's formality lies in its structure and a few basic conventions.

Follow these three guidelines in developing your tone:

Be positive; be definite; be sincere.

Be positive: always say what you *will* do; not what you can't.
We cannot supply the goods before October.
We will send the goods on 1 October.
Be definite: don't make vague promises.
I will try to hold the tickets for you.
I will hold these tickets for three days.
Be sincere: don't hide your meaning behind nice words. Your reader may see through them or misinterpret what you are saying. Try to

generate the feeling appropriate to your purpose. If your message is bad news, there's no point in pretending it's better than it is.

We are looking into your complaint.

Unfortunately, we cannot take action on your complaint.

Salutations

The etiquette of letter-writing has relaxed in recent years. A few basic rules will suffice.

- Use the reader's name if you know it. The form of the name will depend on how they have addressed you or signed themselves, or on how well you know them. Business contacts, even if they have never previously communicated, now increasingly use first names.

Dear Gillian . . .

Dear Freddie . . .

The more formal style of salutation is normally reserved for customers or members of the public.

Dear Mr Callery . . .

Dear Mrs Ikoli . . .

- If the marital status of a female reader is unclear, and you feel you cannot use her first name, convention suggests using Ms.
- If you cannot find out your reader's name, you might use a job title.

Dear Production Manager . . .

Dear Headteacher . . .

- As a last resort, you may have to use:

Dear Sir . . .

Dear Madam . . .

Dear Sir or Madam . . .

But avoid these if at all possible. They are impersonal and unfriendly. They no longer denote a business style; they merely show lack of personal attention to the reader.

Headings

Most business letters benefit from a heading. Go back to your statement of purpose for ideas.

Make sure your heading is short but meaningful. *Invoice 876230* may mean nothing; *Installation of new kitchen units* is more helpful. Place the heading between the salutation and the opening handshake. A heading allows you to start the letter with a short first sentence:

DELIVERIES OF SMOKELESS FUEL
Thank you for your enquiry.

RE: SITING OF STREET LAMPS IN TURL STREET
Many thanks for your helpful remarks.

Continuation pages of long letters should have headers, in case pages are separated. The header should include the addressee's name, the date and the page number. Repeating the letter's main heading could also be useful.

Opening and closing 'handshakes'

Many business conversations begin and end with a 'handshake'. If you would normally shake your reader's hand when you meet them, consider using a handshake to start and finish your letter.

Avoid handshakes that are hackneyed, verbose or old-fashioned. Imagine what you would say at the beginning or end of a professional conversation with your reader, and transcribe that as closely as possible onto the page. You may need to formalize it slightly, but aim for sincerity and warmth rather than stilted convention.

Opening and closing handshakes: *examples*

Many writers find it difficult to think of something original to say as a handshake. Look for something that is appropriate to the particular occasion, purpose and reader.
Many writers open a letter using words they would never use in conversation.
Further to our previous correspondence . . .
I refer to your telephone conversation . . .
I confirm receipt of your letter . . .
With reference to . . .
With regard to . . .

Opening and closing handshakes: *examples – continued*

I am in receipt of your letter . . .
I write further with regard to your complaint.
Try these opening handshakes and see how they might fit your needs. You may be able to adapt one of them; or they might suggest a different set of words.
Thank you for your letter of 4 April.
We spoke on the phone today about . . .
I was interested to read your comments on. . .
I am the new Production Manager at Lavaflow.
It was a pleasure to meet you on. . .
I am concerned about . . .
I am interested in . . .
We met recently at the conference on . . .
I have been investigating your complaint on behalf of GBV Ltd.
Avoid stale and standard closing handshakes:
Assuring you of our best attention . . .
In the meantime, if your have any queries, please do not hesitate to contact me . . .
We trust this clarifies the position.
We trust the above is in order.
We trust this will be of some assistance to you.
These remarks, and others like them, have become such clichés that the reader will not know whether they are genuine or not. You can be polite *and* genuine. Here are some suggestions. Adapt and alter them to suit your needs.
If you have any questions, please contact me on this number during office hours.
Please feel free to telephone me . . .
I look forward to meeting you/receiving your letter/working with you . . .
If I can be of any further help, please contact me on . . .
Please call me on . . . if you need help.
Thank you for your help.
Please reply within 14 days of the date of this letter.
I'm sorry that we cannot be of more help.
I urge you to settle this account now or call me to discuss payment arrangements.
Please do not ignore this letter.
I look forward to hearing from you shortly.

The complimentary close and signature

The rule is simple. Use *Yours sincerely* when you salute the reader by name. Otherwise use *Yours faithfully*. Other complimentary closes will suggest other types of relationship than the strictly professional. Use them at your own risk.

Note the use of capital letters: for *Yours* only.

Sign with your first name if you have saluted the reader by first name; otherwise with your first and last names (not an initial and last name).

Print or type your full name below the signature, including a personal title if you wish (*Mr, Mrs, Miss, Ms*). The job title is printed or typed below the printed name. Name or job title – but not both – can be printed in upper case.

Yours sincerely

Michelle Sussams
PERSONNEL DIRECTOR

Layout and other matters

Most business letters come in one of two layouts:

Indented

– addresses and close/signature progressively indented
– heading, writer's name and job title centred
– closed punctuation (commas and stops in names and addresses, dates, complimentary close).

This is now regarded as old-fashioned, mostly because of the complexity of typing – not recommended.

Blocked

– everything starting at the left margin
– open punctuation (all punctuation omitted outside the main body of the letter).

This is far easier to produce, and is now increasingly accepted as the norm.

INFORMATION FOR BUSINESS
The Wideawake Centre, Sixways, BIRMINGHAM, B98 6CX

Our ref:
Your ref:

6 July 19 . .

Bena Patel
Reader and Reader
Dingley Place
ANYTOWN
Greenshire
AY99 3FR

Dear Bena
The fully blocked layout

Thank you for your letter of 1 July. This is an example of the blocked style of letter you asked about.

As you can see, everything in the letter starts at the left margin. Punctuation is open: only essential dots and commas are included. All this makes the letter much easier and quicker to type.

My own feeling, however, is that fully blocked letters can sometimes look rather lopsided. This impression would be reinforced if I had to type my own name and address above yours at the head of the letter.

Some writers prefer to right-justify: to make a straight margin at the right-hand side. Research suggests that a ragged right margin improves readability. Anyway, I think it looks more personal and less official.

I hope this answers your questions, and that my tone strikes you as friendly. If you would like to discuss matters further, please write to me.

Yours sincerely

Delia Whitbread
Communications Administrator

References

References allow for easy filing and help everybody to keep track of correspondence. They are normally made up of:
- initials of writer (in capitals)
- initials of typist (usually in lower case)
- reference to a particular file, account, invoice, etc. (if relevant).

When replying to a referenced letter, quote both references in the following order:

Our ref: AB/pr/CF4
Your ref: FG/kj

References are usually placed above the date at the head of the letter.

The date

Every letter should be dated, including standard or circular letters. Use a clean, uncluttered form. Commas and stops are not normally used in blocked layout.

Abbreviations (Jan '99) are unsuitable, as are numerical forms of the date: these can cause confusion across cultural barriers. 2/4/99, for example, is 2 April in English and 4 February in American. The recommended date form is *2 April 1999.*

After the close

A few elements sometimes follow the signature and typed name and job title.
- PS – or P.S. – is quite acceptable in business letters. Indeed, it can be a useful way of highlighting a bit of information, or reminding the reader of a small point. The device is particularly common in marketing letters, where it fabricates a friendly, personal tone. Be aware of the effect PS may have and use it carefully.
- Enc., or Encs 3, indicate papers enclosed with the letter. Sometimes a slash (/) is placed in the margin beside the textual reference to the enclosure. A description of the enclosures is helpful.
- Copies of the letter to third parties are indicated by cc, Copy to or Copies to, with relevant names added.

CHAPTER 11

Reports

> **At a glance**
>
> Reports are management tools. A report is an exercise in persuasion, so your report must have a useful message.
> Many reports have a number of readers. The message addresses the primary readership. Write down a function statement to clarify your thinking. Don't confuse your purpose with the report's function. Check that your message addresses the appropriate problem or answers the appropriate question. Check with your primary reader if necessary.
> Use an extended pyramid to present the complicated information that supports the message. Translate the pyramid into an outline, and the outline into a first draft with apparatus to help the reader find their way around.

Reports are management tools. They usually require research, analysis, auditing, investigations, interviews or experimental work; but their readers *use* reports to take action: to make a judgement, form an opinion, decide what to do, improve a procedure, create policy...

A report is an exercise in persuasion. At the very least, you must persuade the reader that what you are telling them is true. But you must also make the truth relevant to them. Above all, you must make it useful.

So your report must have something to say. Like any other functional document, it must deliver *one* message. Finding that message may be difficult. You may not know what you want to say until you have completed your research. Your message may be the conclusion you reach, or the recommendation that you want to make as a result of your research.

Categories of reader

Many reports will have a number of readers. Creating a clear message can be difficult if you feel that you must address them all equally. Categorize your readership to make the job easier.

Every report will have *primary* readers. They will put it to immediate use. They may have commissioned it. If they don't read the report, there will have been no point in writing it. If you have more than one primary reader, there must be *one* clear reason that binds them together: perhaps they all need to agree to the proposal; perhaps they are all users or customers.

- Who is your primary reader?
- How many are there? What common factor connects them?
- What do you want them to do?
- What do they need to know in order to do what you want them to do?

Secondary readers may use your report by relating it to their own work, or by extracting detailed information for some other purpose. Your line manager may be a secondary reader: perhaps they have asked you to write the report, and you may have to submit it for their approval before circulation; it may even go out in their name. The primary reader, however, could be someone else.

- How do your secondary readers differ from the primary readers?
- What different uses will they make of the report? Can you accommodate all their needs in the one document?
- What information will they need? Can you include it all? How (appendices, annexes, attachments)?

Tertiary readers include people you'll never meet, or even know about: managers 'up the line', or in other departments. The tertiary readership may change over time. Other people in other organizations may come to read your report; it may be sent elsewhere or even be quietly 'borrowed'. It may lie in a file or archive, appearing years later in somebody else's work.

- Do you have any idea of a tertiary readership?
- Can you guess how they might use the report?
- Will your report be stored or filed? Where? Why?
- How could you make your report understandable to these unknown people?

Writing a function statement

Writing down your report's function will help you clarify your thinking. If writing this statement is difficult, you may need to discuss and agree it with the person who has asked for the report.

The function statement is in two parts:

- the first part ('The aim of this report is to ...') expresses the report's immediate aim: what you and the primary reader (or 'client') want it to do
- the second part ('so that ...') looks to the *future*. What benefit, payoff or action do you see as a result of producing the report? Think in terms of broad objectives: words like 'maximize', 'minimize' or 'optimize' (meaning 'make best use of') may be useful.

Function statement

The aim of this report is to _____

_____ (What is the report's immediate task?)

so that _____

_____ (Expected payoff or benefit)

Signature of writer ....

Signature of client ....

Date ....

Function statements can help the writer and user of the report to agree its purpose. This will help to guard against producing an inappropriate or irrelevant report. If events overtake you – if the client's needs or your objectives change – revise the function statement to forestall confusion and unnecessary arguments.

Your purpose and the report's function

Writers often confuse their own purpose with the function of the report itself.

A report cannot think. So it can't:

- find out
- get something done
- research
- review
- ask

- determine
- analyse
- explore
- evaluate
- choose.

These are all legitimate aims for you, the writer. They cannot be the function of your report. If your purpose was to find out or research, how is your report going to use the results of that work? For example, your purpose may be to analyse a set of figures; your report's purpose may be to use the results to support an argument, to demonstrate a trend, to explain how something affects something else, to lay out a set of options for action . . .

Checking the message

Nothing is more important than the report's message. Everything else – the information you include, the order you put it in, the structure you create – depends on the message.

Because the message is so important, check carefully that it is saying exactly what you want to say. Is the message appropriate to your primary reader? Could you say it more simply, or assertively? What form of words will *sell* the report to the reader?

SPQR: *situation / problem / question / response*

Check your message by telling yourself a story about how the need for your report arose.

SITUATION

The *situation* is the first thing you can say about the matter under consideration that your reader will agree is true. It is the equivalent to 'Once upon a time': an uncontroversial starting point.

PROBLEM

The *problem* arises within the situation to alter it. Problems can be either *presented* or *constructed*. Presented problems are obstacles, beyond our control or responsibility. They include:

- something that has gone wrong
- something that could go wrong
- a discrepancy between expectations and results
- a change in circumstances beyond our control
- a possible change in the situation.

Constructed problems are those we make for ourselves. We may want to know how to:

- do something
- plan for what might happen
- improve the way we do something
- do something different
- review the options for action
- understand everybody's point of view.

You and your primary reader may have very different ideas about what the problem is.

QUESTION

What question did the problem trigger in the *client's* mind?

RESPONSE

Your response to that question should be the same as the message of your report.

Many reports tackle the wrong problem or answer the wrong question. Work out SPQR from the primary reader's point of view. Check with your primary reader that you are tackling the right problem or answering the right question.

Checking the message: *example*

Imagine you are writing a report about improving the efficiency of product distribution. As you understand it, SPQR would look like this:

SITUATION
We distribute products.

PROBLEM
Our distribution process is inefficient.

QUESTION
Can we improve the efficiency of our distribution process?

RESPONSE
We can distribute products more efficiently.
or
We can improve the efficiency of product distribution in three ways.
or even
We cannot improve the efficiency of product distribution.
Which response you choose will depend on what you have discovered in your research. But these three messages are all inappropriate:
We need to make product distribution more efficient.
I have investigated the efficiency of product distribution.
This report analyses areas of possible improvement in product distribution.

The first simply restates the problem. The second fatally confuses the writer's purpose with the report's function. And the third describes the document's function rather than expressing it.

Extending the pyramid

A report presents complicated information. Your task is to make complexity simple. Planning the report, then, is a matter of creating a structure that progressively summarizes detailed information.

You do this by building an extended pyramid. A pyramid supports a message with a few pieces of information (or *key points*). Your message should provoke a question in the reader's mind. The question is one of three:

Why?, How? or Which?

The key points are your answers to that question. You must have at least two key points; try to have no more than about six.

Each of the key points, in turn, provokes a question that you answer with a small number of *sub-points*. Again, each key point must be supported by at least two, and no more than about six, sub-points. These create another level of the pyramid. You might even create another level of information by supporting some sub-points with *minor points*.

The best way to work out this extended pyramid is as a diagram. A pictorial version of your pyramid allows you to see whether your thinking is clear.

Once complete, the sentences in your pyramid should obey three rules.

1. Every sentence should be a summary of the sentences grouped beneath it.
2. All the sentences in a group should be answers to the question provoked by the summarizing sentence.
3. Sentences in a group should be ordered logically. The order might be:
   - chronological (events in time, steps in a process)
   - structural (into sets, categories or items in a list)
   - comparative (biggest to smallest, most important to least important)
   - logical (steps in an argument: this is true, this is also true, therefore . . .).

Building an extended pyramid: *example*

A report's pyramid extends in an internally consistent way. Each point summarizes the points gathered at the level beneath. This report pyramid is in three layers. Complicated documents might extend to four, but no more.

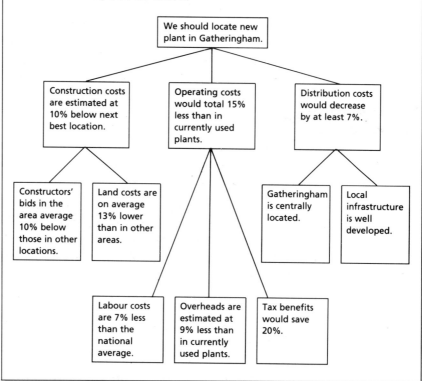

The pyramid diagram allows you to see your report in miniature, on one sheet of paper. Building it disciplines your thinking: you can see what pieces of information you need, where they go and how they relate to other pieces of information.

Writing an outline

Translate your pyramid of information into an outline. This is the skeleton of the report. You can show the outline to your reader as work in progress; if anything needs changing, it's easier to see and alter an outline than pages of text.

- Place your message at the head of a sheet of paper. Add the heading: 'SUMMARY'.
- Translate SPQR into a *very few* sentences and place it immediately following the summary. Head this 'INTRODUCTION'.
- Next, place your key points in order down the page, numbering them but omitting headings for the moment.
- Add sub-points under each main point, indenting and numbering them to indicate clearly their status.
- Repeat the process, if necessary, for minor points.

Report outline: *example*

SUMMARY
We should locate new plant in Gatheringham.

INTRODUCTION
Our business is rapidly expanding. Existing manufacturing plant will reach capacity within three years. We urgently need to decide where to locate new manufacturing plant. This report recommends the Gatheringham area and justifies the recommendation in strategic terms.

1. Construction costs in Gatheringham are estimated at 10% below those of the next best location.
    1.1 Constructors' bids in the area average 10% below those in other locations.
    1.2 Land costs are on average 13% lower than in other areas.

2. Operating costs would total 15% less than in current plants.
    2.1 Labour costs are 7% less than the national average.
    2.2 Overheads are estimated at 9% less than in current plants.
    2.3 The tax package would save 20%.

3. Distribution costs would decrease by at least 7%.
    3.1 Gatheringham is centrally located.
    3.2 The local infrastructure is well developed.

Producing a first draft

Turn the outline into a first draft by adding flesh to the report's skeleton. Follow the plan and numbering of your outline exactly.

You will fill out the outline by adding:

- text
- figures (pictures, graphics, diagrams)
- headings and sub-headings.

Your report will also contain apparatus to help your reader find their way around. These navigation aids include the title page, contents list, appendices, section numbering and page numbering. Give them careful attention. All help to 'sell' the document to your reader.

Main sections of a report

Follow this order when laying out your report. Each section should start on a new page. Some reports will exclude the items *in italics*.
Title page
Summary
Contents list
Figures list
Introduction
Main sections
Glossary of terms
Bibliography
References
Appendices
Index

Summary or introduction?

Report writers often confuse the functions of the summary and introduction. Outlining should make the distinction clear.

The *summary* contains the whole report in miniature. The essence of the summary is your message. Place the summary at the very front of the report – immediately following the title page – and the message at the very head of the summary. Support the message with key points and, if necessary, with sub-points. You could, of course, use the outline as a ready-made summary of your report.

The *introduction* explains how the report came into being. The essence of the introduction is SPQR: background information including the problem addressed by the report and the question it answers. In the first draft, the introduction might expand to include methodology, acknowledgements, and even a potted guide to the main sections of the report.

Numbering systems

Different writers and organizations favour different numbering systems in reports. Some use letters for main sections; others use Roman numbers (I, II, III . . . or i, ii, iii . . .); some use numbers on one level and letters on another.

My own choice is a decimal numbering system using only Arabic numbers. This system clarifies for the reader at a glance the levels of the information: 1.1 is obviously a sub-section of section 1, 1.1.1 a minor section, and so on. This numbering system is neat, unobtrusive and easy to understand.

CHAPTER 12

Instructions and procedures

At a glance

Instructions and procedures explain how something happens.
More and more are being written at work.
The worst sin in procedural writing is to ignore the reader. How
will they use the document? Consider organizing it by user
activity rather than by technical specification. What is the
relevance of the instruction to the reader? What is the assumed
level of expertise? How will the reader best understand the
procedure?
'Chunking' makes procedures easier to follow by breaking the
process into steps. Use a template including:
- overview
- steps in the process
- explanations of each step.

Use headings that clearly indicate what is in each section.
Experiment with unusual styles of heading.
Use simple orders rather than tortuous passive constructions.
Don't worry that using commands may seem aggressive. Your
reader wants to be instructed, not flattered.
Navigation markers and graphics can make the document more
effective.

Instructions and procedures explain how something happens. *Instructions* tell the user or operator exactly how to do something. *Procedures* give a less detailed overview of a process, often to satisfy an audit or quality requirement. Standard Operating Procedures (SOPs) usually document all the regular activities of a department or team. They may need to conform to a British or international standard.

More and more procedural documents are being written at work. The most obvious examples are instructions for IT users. Other kinds of procedural documents include staff handbooks, office bibles, health and safety instructions and manuals of all kinds.

Instructions and procedures have a wide audience, many of whom may not have yet joined the organization. You will need to think about:

- how much detail to include
- how to lay out the material for easiest use
- how to explain complicated options or special conditions.

Targeting the user

The worst sin in procedural writing is to ignore the user. IT manuals are notorious for doing this. They explain *everything* the machine or software will do, although most users will only want to do a few of them. Beware of falling into the same trap. Think of a procedure from the user's point of view. If you are instructing them how to use equipment, concentrate on how the user will use the equipment rather than its *features*.

How will the reader use the document? An instruction will be handled repeatedly, perhaps in a dirty or hostile environment. Operating procedures may be read more rarely, and may need to be more formally produced. If there is a range of activities, can you categorize them by user groups? Do the activities fall into a logical sequence?

Consider organizing the material entirely by user activity rather than by technical specification. This may mean dividing the document into sections by user group, or aligning the instruction with other processes the user already knows. Conditions of use will also suggest certain kinds of typeface and point sizes. What kind of paper (or screen format) is most appropriate? You may need to use plastic-coated paper or protective covers.

What is the relevance of the instruction to the reader? They may have to be able to read the instructions easily in an emergency. Health and safety instructions, for example, must be immediately accessible. You may have to sell other kinds of instruction in different ways. Your user may be hostile to a new procedure, or to the idea of another initiative from Head Office. You may have to write a covering document that sells the *benefits* of the new procedure to the user.

What is the assumed level of expertise? Are you writing for a novice, or a hardened professional? Your readership will probably include a wide spectrum of experience.

Structure the process in layers. Experts need then read only the essential instructions, and beginners can 'drill down' to more detailed instructions. On paper, this layering could be reflected in the layout on the page, by different typefaces, etc. In electronic documents, different levels can remain hidden until revealed through an icon.

How will the reader best understand the procedure? You may be writing within an established convention of procedural writing: you may even have to use templates or forms. Your user may be accustomed to digesting information in a certain way: lists of equipment in one part of the document, step-by-step instructions in another. You may need to include new or specialized terms in a glossary. Keep your language simple. If you suspect that the reader won't understand a term, you must define it. Map your terms one-to-one to the equipment to avoid confusion. For example, if you refer to a 'red button', make sure you mean exactly the same red button each time.

Creating a useful structure

'Chunking' is an essential element of any clear procedure. Nobody will read a procedure that isn't immediately easy to follow. If the key steps are buried inside long paragraphs, or clogged by complicated language, the reader will simply give up – and start to make mistakes. Number the chunks to make them clear.

This template works well for many different kinds of procedure:

- overview: the process as a whole, in context
- steps in the process: broken into large and small steps if necessary
- explanations of each step: including warnings, special conditions, and so on.

A recipe is the most obvious example of a procedure organized in this way. The overview is a brief description of the dish and the list of ingredients; the steps appear as numbered paragraphs; explanations of particular skills or conditions are added at the end. Analysing recipes is a useful source of ideas for writing other kinds of procedures.

Overview

This should act as a summary of the procedure. The overview explains the purpose of the process and its context: the conditions under which it will operate, any procedures that must be complete before this one starts, what processes follow, and the relationship of this procedure to others. The overview might also include more detailed technical information. The procedure may need specific equipment, or ingredients, prepared in a particular way. The user may need to use special skills, or watch out for critical signs or conditions.

Steps in the process

Break the process into a *small* number of steps. No procedure should need more than about six steps to explain it at a certain level of simplicity. Explain more complicated procedures on two levels: the major steps, and the minor steps within each major one. Layering the steps is probably the most useful technique in making the procedure clear to the reader. Number the steps, both major and minor. Arabic numbers work best for the major steps (1, 2, 3, ...); use decimal numbers for the minor steps to show unambiguously where they belong (1.1, 1.2, 1.3, ...; 2.1, 2.2, 2.3, ...).

Explanations of each step

This is a separate section explaining the instructions in more detail and showing how to get from one step to the next. Use the same numbering here as for the list of steps itself. Include warnings about special conditions, danger spots, moments where special skill or attention is necessary and tips for getting better results. There's no harm in repeating some of these from the overview.

Headings

The headings and sub-headings in the document should clearly indicate what is in each section. Beware headings that are too general, or too wordy. Headings should not merely label but actively predict what's coming.

LABEL HEADINGS	PREDICTIVE HEADINGS
Filing	*How to file invoices*
Storage facilities	*Where to store construction materials*
Electrical shock	*How to treat electric shock*

Experiment with unusual styles of heading, such as questions.

What do I do to . . .?
How do I stop . . .?

Style

The most important element of style in instructions is the simple command – known grammatically as the imperative. Such verbs emphasize the action strongly and early in the sentence: the reader knows exactly what to do. Many writers, perhaps out of politeness, shy away from using orders. Instead, they clog the text with passive verbs, which lengthen the sentences and make the action far less clear.

Using the imperative: *example*

Here is a typical paragraph from a procedural document. Passive verbs appear in **bold**.

*All internal documents **are to be filed** electronically, whereas documents leaving the company **will be filed** in paper files. When an internal document **is filed** electronically, all paper copies **will be binned** or, if comments **have been included**, the comments **are to be entered** in brief onto the electronic copy before the paper copy **is destroyed**.*

Nearly all of these passive verbs can become imperatives – simple commands. Placing them at the start of sentences and numbering the steps of the process makes the whole passage much easier to understand. Imperatives appear in **bold**.

File *all internal documents electronically.* **File** *copies of documents leaving the company in paper files.*

Bin *all paper copies of documents stored electronically.* **Enter** *any comments from internal documents on the electronic copy before destroying the paper copy.*

Don't worry that using commands may seem aggressive. Instructions are meant to order the reader, not flatter them. The word 'please' can be effective sometimes to make an instruction more palatable to a customer or user. If you suspect that the reader may be hostile to this new procedure, you must persuade them of its benefits *before* instructing them. A covering note or report may be necessary to convince them.

Other elements of style make procedures more effective. Navigation markers will help your document to be more user-friendly: an attractive title page and list of contents, summaries and boxes, a question and answer format. A sanserif font may look more friendly and less official; a larger typeface may be useful for visually impaired readers. Maybe you could lay out the material as a brochure or leaflet, or use foldouts for glossaries or illustrations.

Graphics

Illustrations or graphics are useful to make technical names clear. A process may be easier to understand when displayed as a table or flow chart, especially if it involves options or loops. Boxes can categorize activities.

Keep your graphics simple. A table or flow chart, for example, shouldn't contain more than a few elements. The reader should be able to read it without using a magnifying glass. Illustrations should be accurate and uncluttered. Make sure that the graphic will still work when scaled down to fit a leaflet or brochure. Use a consistent scale so that parts maintain their relative proportions. Position illustrations with the text so that page turns are kept to a minimum.

The best way to test an instruction or procedure is to ask somebody to use it. Give the document to a user or group of users – preferably not a close colleague – and watch how they interpret it. Don't intervene unless they ask for help (if they do, the instruction may be failing). Ask them how clear they found the document, identify particular misinterpretations and redraft the document as necessary.

CHAPTER 13

Agendas and minutes

At a glance

Agendas and minutes are both part of the overall process of administering a meeting. Hold a pre-meeting meeting to establish the meeting's purpose, who will attend, what kind of minutes are needed and how the minute-taker can take more responsibility.

An agenda is a list of things to be done: a list of instructions for the participants. Include timings and avoid 'Any other business' if possible.

Minutes are a brief summary of events; not a verbatim record of what people said. They should follow the agenda exactly. Use a note-taking method that allows you to listen well. Identify the important points by listening through what people say to the key ideas. Intervene to clarify and summarize.

Construct each minute simply: background, discussion, decision, action. Avoid 'minutespeak' by cutting down on reported speech, passive verbs and awkward tenses.

Good minute-takers are worth their weight in gold. All too often, though, they are called in without warning and asked to record a meeting without knowing its objectives, or even what the participants are talking about. If nobody can be found to take minutes, the Chair may have to take on the responsibility in addition to running the meeting.

Effective minutes depend a good deal on effective agendas. Writing both is properly part of the overall process of administering a meeting. Along with the Chair, the Meeting Administrator is the most important person involved. Hold a pre-meeting meeting between Chair and Administrator. Use it as an opportunity to clarify some essential points.

- *Why* the meeting is being held: its purpose; and why it is necessary.
- *Who* will attend (and who will not); their function in the meeting, and how they will contribute; who is the Chair and who will take minutes.
- *When* the meeting will be held; when it will finish; how long each item will take; and times of breaks.
- *Where* the meeting will be held; where people will sit; whether any special equipment is required; and where the minute-taker will sit (where they can *see* everybody's face; *not* in the corner!).
- *What* the meeting will be about; the order of the items; what terminology will be used, and what it means; and what kind of minutes are needed.

Unless you answer these questions now, the meeting is likely to be over-long, confused, and unproductive. Establish your right, as the minute taker, to intervene during the meeting: to clarify procedure, decisions and agreed actions.

The agenda

The immediate result of the pre-meeting meeting is the agenda. Circulate this about seven days in advance of the meeting. Sometimes a draft agenda circulates for comments and is then revised.

The word 'agenda' is Latin for 'things to be done'. An agenda is not merely a list of headings. It is a list of instructions for the participants in the meeting. Its tasks are:

- to give advance warning to all participants
- to state the purpose of the meeting
- to indicate what preparation is required
- to give the order of items
- to help the Chair (and others) control the meeting
- to help the minute-taker write up the minutes.

All agendas should include:

- the venue, date and time of the meeting
- the name of the meeting, indicating its purpose
- apologies for absence
- the read and agreed minutes of the previous meeting
- matters arising from those minutes
- items in the main part of the meeting
- the venue, date and time of the next meeting (including the all-important: 'Please bring your diary')
- the time the meeting ends.

No meeting, or part of a meeting, should last more than 90 minutes. Build in breaks, with refreshments if necessary. The items on the agenda should be brief, specific and action-centred. Allocate to each item a length of time. The procedure for each item should be clear (a presentation; a guest speaker; discussing a report; making a decision) and the 'owner' of the item should be identified. The order of items can be crucial to the meeting's success. Put urgent but quick items first, longer items for discussion later.

Avoid 'Any other business'. It is an invitation for the meeting to go out of control, when it should be drawing to a close. Participants use it as a pretext for old grudges and to settle old scores – sometimes even to hijack the meeting. If something is worth discussing, include it as an item on the agenda. If a draft agenda circulates to all participants, they have no excuse for complaint that an important matter is missing. In a real emergency, the Chair can amend the agenda at the beginning of the meeting.

Constructing an agenda: *example*

TEAM MEETING

Conference room, 3 September, 9.00 am – 10.30 am

To attend: Richard Newcombe (Chair)
Sue Rogerson (Administrator and minute-taker)
Steve Josephs
Deirdre Robbins
Brian Smith

Constructing an agenda: *example – continued*

1 **Individual achievements over the last quarter:**   **10 mins**
   Richard to report and announce 'team member
   of the quarter'

2 **Improving our expenses paperwork:**   **5 mins**
   Deirdre to update on new procedures and provide
   examples

3 **Stationery cupboard – maintenance rota:**   **10 mins**
   Steve to announce new procedure for maintaining
   stocks and keeping the cupboard in good order

4 **Client opportunities – new sectors:**   **15 mins**
   Brian to announce results of market research, with
   discussion

5 **Team strategy:**   **45 mins**
   Richard to propose strategy for next quarter:
   in-depth discussion leading to identification and
   agreement of objectives

6 **Date and time of next meeting (please bring your diaries)**

Minutes

The very word 'minutes' suggests something brief: a summary of events. Minutes are a record of what happened at the meeting: the key issues, decisions and agreed actions. They do *not* need to record what people said. The term 'verbatim minutes' is a contradiction in terms. A record of every word spoken requires a tape-recorder or stenographer: the result is a transcript, like *Hansard*.

Minutes perform a number of vital functions:
- a permanent record of what happened
- evidence for legal or professional reasons
- a reminder of actions to be done
- an aid in writing the next agenda.

All minutes should follow the agenda exactly. They should include:
- the name of the meeting
- the venue, date and time

- names of participants
- 'Apologies for absence'
- where necessary, 'Minutes read agreed and signed'
- where necessary, 'Matters arising'
- a record of the meeting, item by item, numbered exactly as on the agenda
- a wide left margin, and a column of about a third of a page width on the right
- actions noted and highlighted in the right-hand column, with names and deadlines
- the date of writing and at least one signature. Usually the minutes are signed by minute-taker and Chair.

There are two skills in producing good minutes:

- taking notes during the meeting
- writing up the minutes after the meeting.

The best method of note-taking is the one that allows you to listen attentively. A *minute book*, hard-backed and A4 size, works like this:

1. Each item on the agenda has a separate page.
2. Each page is ruled into three columns: the central one is half the width of the page.
3. Column 1 for names of speakers
   Column 2 for key words of the discussion
   Column 3 for actions and information.
4. Minutes in *note form*. Leave at least half a page space at the end of each item for late additions.
5. Actions in Column 3, perhaps using different colours to highlight. Include deadlines and names or initials of person responsible for the actions. *Information* is material to be passed on to people not at the meeting.

Listening to a meeting

Identifying the important points in a complex and often chaotic conversation requires skill and concentration. Resist writing down the words people speak; try always to distil the essential point they are making from the mass of language that you can hear.

Listen *through* the words for important information: data, ideas. Listen for actions performed, suggested or agreed. What has changed – or not changed? Listening becomes easier if you can intervene to check your understanding of what you have heard. You may need to agree these actions with the Chair.

- Intervene within items to clarify points that are unclear.
- Summarize at the end of each item, so that the group can reflect on what it has achieved.

Summarizing a discussion

- Why is the matter being discussed?
- What has happened? Who has been responsible?
- What has *not* been done?
- What has changed since the matter was last discussed?
- What will be done? By whom? When? Where?
- Who else is involved?

Constructing minutes

The format and style of your minutes are dictated in part by what your Chair wants, and by the conventions of your organization. Some committees expect lengthy, discursive minutes (though they may not read them). Others demand only a list of action points. Team meetings in fast-moving companies increasingly produce minutes as a spreadsheet, with one line per agenda item and cells for the action agreed, actioner and deadline. They are completed during the meeting and distributed by e-mail as the meeting closes.

Be guided by how minutes have appeared in the past, but be prepared also to improve wherever you can. These guidelines should help.

Using your notes, try to distil your minute into a single message. This might be a record of what the group achieved, of what people agreed to do, or simply what happened at that point in the meeting. *The meeting agreed a pricing strategy for the next twelve months.*

The committee agreed to review staffing levels in the light of increased customer demand.

The team discussed parking arrangements at Headquarters.
Now group the main points under your message in four sections.

Background

Put the item in context for anybody who was not at the meeting. The title of the item may do the job; otherwise, indicate very briefly how the matter arose.

Discussion

How much to include? Don't attribute statements to named individuals unless they ask you to. Include references to what has or hasn't happened or changed, objectives, new circumstances that affect the group's thinking. Where necessary, include recent events, dates and names of places or people, sums of money and any legal or contractual matters.

Decision

A summary of what has been agreed.

Action

What is to be done? By whom? When and where? Highlight actions by placing them in a separate paragraph or in a column on the right-hand side, using bold type as appropriate.

Improving the style

Many writers become afflicted with 'minutespeak' when they produce their meeting notes. Keep paragraphs short – no more than about four or five lines each – and your sentences brief. Three other elements of style are particularly important:

- reported speech
- passive verbs
- tense.

Reported speech

Minutes should not be a record of everything people said at a meeting. Try not to overuse verbs to do with talking.

said	*asked*
reported	*discussed*
explained	*proposed*
suggested	*expressed*
confirmed	*requested*
introduced	*stated*
remarked	*observed*
emphasized	*stressed*
spoke	*mentioned*

Unless a participant asks you to record a specific remark, concentrate on background, issues, decisions and actions.

Passive verbs

Passive verbs are the main reason why minutes are so often unreadable. Often they come with empty subjects.

It was questioned whether . . .
It was thought necessary to . . .
It was reported that . . .
It was stated that . . .

As you don't need to record what people say anyway, many passive verbs (including all those listed above) can disappear. Convert others into active verbs to make your minutes crisper, clearer and more dynamic.

It was agreed that . . .	*The committee agreed . . .*
The resolution was not passed.	*We could not pass the resolution.*
The plans were considered.	*The meeting considered the plans.*

Tense

The words 'would', 'could' and 'should' also tend to clog up minutes: a result of the traditional 'rule' that minutes should always be in the past tense.

It makes sense to record what happened at the meeting in the past tense.

Tom presented a report on current car fleet usage.

Using past tenses throughout, however, creates an unnatural and cumbersome style.

Tom presented a report on current car fleet usage. He revealed that some sales staff had still been claiming for unreasonably high mileage figures. After some discussion, it was agreed that Tom would continue to monitor expense forms and would report back to the committee at the next meeting.

Remember that, as the minutes are dated, the present tense is quite acceptable for ongoing actions or opinions.

Some sales staff are still claiming for unreasonably high mileage figures.

Use the future for agreed actions.

Tom will continue to monitor expense forms and report back at the next meeting.

The resulting minute is still accurate, far more brief and crystal clear.

Of course, you need not use full sentences in minutes. Abbreviated notes are often just as effective and can dispense with the problem tense at a stroke – as long as your meaning is still clear.

Tom's report: current car fleet usage. Continued unreasonable mileage claims from some sales staff. Tom to continue to monitor forms and report back.

CHAPTER 14

Managing others' writing

At a glance

Managing others' writing is important and delicate work. Some managers refuse to alter a word that their staff write; others thoroughly revise every document. Few seem to do more than make corrections.

The idea of correction can be damaging. Some managers correct in the quest for a standard style. Corporate style, however, is often a polite name for bad habits. Improving anybody's style may mean chipping away the layers of corporate style.

Good management of writing begins and ends with establishing ownership of the work. Writing is very much a task for an individual. Help others to improve by developing their skills and giving them workable standards.

Coaching helps people think for themselves by encouraging awareness and responsibility. Telling, instructing or ordering are only minimally effective. Coach primarily by asking questions. Use the GROW coaching model. Set Goals; analyse Reality; generate Options for improvement; agree What to do.

Coach the team by involving them in establishing the standards of clear and effective writing and by offering your own work for inspection. Lead by example.

Managing others' writing is important work. Your team will be judged on the quality of their writing. The documents you send create an image of you and your organization in your readers' minds. Irritating mistakes, an unfortunate tone and poor presentation all give a poor impression. They may even lead to serious misunderstandings.

It's a delicate matter. Writing is both a highly technical skill and an intensely personal activity. Many managers tackle the challenge of developing somebody's writing skills by taking one of two options: 'hands off' or 'hands on'.

Some managers refuse to alter any letter or report their staff produce. They feel, understandably, that each writer should take full responsibility for what they write.

Asking people to take responsibility without developing their skills, however, is unhelpful.

Others thoroughly rewrite every document that crosses their desk. Perhaps it's a way of making their mark. But imposing your style on everybody's work sends a clear message that only one style will do. Your team will try to copy your style rather than trying to improve their own. Apart from wasting time on matters that shouldn't be their responsibility, the 'hands on' approach can leave staff feeling frustrated and resentful.

Putting it right

Few managers seem to do more than change the work their staff produce. They may say that time is lacking to do more. 'Red-penning' by itself, though, is never satisfactory. It can confuse, demoralize and do considerable damage to your reputation as a manager.

Four main complaints emerge from writers about the way managers alter their work.

- *The idea of correction*. Altering a piece of writing is invariably seen as 'correcting' it, by both manager and writer. Of course, grammar, punctuation and spelling must be correct – or at least not glaringly wrong. But choosing words is not just a question of correctness; it's also a matter of choice and personal taste. The writer, however, may not see it that way: to them, whatever you change must be wrong; whatever you suggest must be right. So they try to imitate your style, rather than developing their own.
- *Continual correction*. If everything people write comes back smothered in red pen, they quickly become demotivated. What's the point of trying to write better if the boss changes it all anyway? Continual correction wears people down and breeds resentment.
- *Contradictory correction*. Managers often 'correct' language differently on different occasions. The writer becomes confused about

what is expected of them, what the standards are, or what is 'correct'.

- *Incorrect correction*. Worst of all, a 'correction' may be wrong. If you are going to put someone right, you need to be certain that you know what's correct. Standards of grammatical correctness change; standards of clear and business-like writing are altering even more quickly. Many of the most common 'corrections' are based on rules and habits half-remembered or misunderstood from school-days or from corporate style guides.

To manage others' writing well, distinguish clearly between issues of correctness and issues of style. Try to move beyond the habit of 'correcting'.

Corporate style

Managers often correct in the quest for a standard style. They try to establish a 'corporate style', which they then publish in a 'Style Guide'. This usually combines instructions about layout and [much more vague] guidelines about language use.

Corporate style is usually a polite name for bad habits. It builds up and petrifies over time. People copy what they read around them, just as they copy the way colleagues speak. The result is a rigid, bureaucratic or technical prose that is difficult to read, hard to understand and deadly dull.

Organizationspeak

A number of factors may contribute to your writing style at work. Do you recognize any of these in your own situation?

- If you lack confidence, you may hide behind familiar words rather than trying to use them well.
- You pick up words and phrases from colleagues or senior managers.
- Pressure of time makes it difficult to improve or do things differently.
- You may have learnt the dangerous lesson that complicated language often impresses people.
- You may have been educated in a specialism that has a private language, making it hard to write in a more public way.

Improving your writing style often means chipping away the layers of corporate style so that you can find your own voice.

Whose writing is it anyway?

Good management of writing begins and ends with the question of ownership. Intervention can easily become hijacking. The writer becomes a passive spectator while you, the manager, assume ownership of the task.

Writing is very much a job for an individual. It involves making complex choices, which are best made by one person. Ideally, responsibility should stay with the person whose name appears as writer. Any interventions by you as a manager should be on that basis: responsibility for choosing what to put rests with them. Of course, responsibility may transfer from one person to another. A report, for example, could be written in sections by a team and edited by one person. A letter may be drafted by a member of your team for you to polish.

Helping others to improve means developing their skills and giving them workable standards by which to judge their own progress.

- Establish your own standards of effective writing.
- Coach individuals and teams.

By establishing clear standards of quality, you can clarify just what you expect from your team (and from yourself). By coaching individuals and teams, you can help people to develop their own taste and judgement.

Setting standards

If you set standards, everyone knows what to aim for. The best standards are those that help people to develop their skills. The standards you set for effective writing need to be specific – so that people can measure or clearly evaluate their work against them – without being too prescriptive or limiting. Standards also help you to coach others. They provide objective criteria that prevent coaching from becoming a battle of opinions.

Establishing standards of effective writing

The guidelines of Plain English are a good place to start in setting your standards.

Here is a suggested list of standards for effective writing. Use them as the basis of your own guidelines. *Do not regard them as rules.*

- Make your average sentence length 15 to 20 words.
- No sentence should contain more than 25 words.
- Prefer short words to long words.
- Use words that your reader is most likely to understand.
- Use as few words as possible.
- Write personally. Use 'I', 'we', 'you' and names whenever you can.
- Use strong, clear and specific verbs. Prefer active verbs to passive.
- Use standard paragraphs or documents as little as possible.

Coaching individuals

Coaching, at its best, empowers people. It gives them the tools to improve their work. People can only motivate themselves. Telling, instructing or ordering remove ownership of the task from the writer. Your role as coach is to help the writer make more informed choices. Coaching depends on establishing a partnership. The coach needs detachment, integrity, support, patience, genuine interest in the coachee and an ability to listen well.

Coaching has the twin aims of building *awareness* and fostering *responsibility*. Building awareness means helping the coachee to see:

- what the document is doing
- the standards of excellence
- the possibilities for improvement
- the options for action.

Building responsibility means encouraging the coachee to decide what to do – both with the document under discussion and, more generally, with documents in the future.

Coaching also helps you, the coach, to learn. It should enable you to challenge your own assumptions, values and beliefs. Coaching is a good opportunity to re-examine your own approach to writing and expand your own skills. At its best, coaching is a dialogue resulting in mutual learning.

The four stages of coaching

The coaching process has four stages, best remembered by the acronym GROW.

- *Goal setting:* establishing what the writer wants to achieve with the document.
- *Reality analysis:* evaluating how well the document achieves this purpose, identifying elements that work well and those that need improvement.
- *Options:* generating possible ways of improving the text.
- *What to do:* identifying how to adjust the text and improve it.

Goal setting involves identifying with the coachee what they want to achieve with the document. Encourage the coachee to identify these goals for themselves. Challenge any goal that you don't under-stand or feel you disagree with – by asking questions as much as possible.

Reality analysis means looking coolly at what the coachee has achieved with the document and where it falls short of achieving what they want. Evaluate the text against the coachee's own goals. Try not to change anything simply to fit your own taste.

Objective standards are useful, because personal choice and opinion can cloud evaluation. Criteria by which to evaluate the document can include:

- the simple templates for letters or other documents offered in this book
- maximum sentence length of 25 words throughout the document
- maximum sentence length of 15 words for the message, topic sentences and other keypoints
- overuse of long words
- overuse of passive verbs

- lack of personal pronouns
- unnecessary words or phrases.

Be sensitive at this stage. Take the exploration slowly. If you find mistakes, avoid pointing them all out at once. Remember that a lot of reality is inner. Ask the coachee how he/she is feeling, whether the conversation is helpful, whether he/she thinks your comments are reasonable. Show that you understand the delicacy of the situation. The coachee may be concealing some of his/her feelings. Prickliness or hostility may conceal very private feelings of inadequacy. He/she may be battling against a long-held sense of educational underachievement, or against dyslexia.

Finding the *options* for action is potentially the most creative part of coaching. Your goal here is to generate a number of ways of improving the text – not simply to find one 'right' answer. Recognize that 'the opponent in your own head' can act as a powerful censor.

Deciding *what to do* means drawing up a clear plan. This is a good point to re-establish ownership of the task. Emphasize that the final choices are the coachee's.

The essence of coaching is asking questions. Questions help the coachee to learn by focusing attention and promoting active involvement. Coachees help you to understand how they are thinking: their priorities, taste and feelings. Questions of this kind are especially important when coaching writing, where technical elements of grammar, punctuation or spelling must be corrected or instructed. Don't underestimate the value of showing somebody what's wrong; but always try to put people right in the context of asking them what they want to achieve.

Key coaching questions

Goal setting
What is the purpose or function of this document?
What do you want it to do?
What do you want to achieve?
Who is the reader?

Key coaching questions – *continued*

What do you want them to do?
Are there specific action points?
What message do you want to give the reader?
What key points do you want to make to support it?

Reality analysis
How have you tried to achieve your goals?
Where is the message?
How well do you think the document does what you want it to do?
How would you react to the document if you were the reader?
Would the reader be clear what to do?

Options
What could you write here?
Can you think of something else?
What do you think about this idea?
Can you use fewer words?
Is there a simpler way of saying it?
Can you find other ways of doing this?

What to do
Do you think you can take this away and finish the job?
Is anything unclear?
Is there anything more I can do to help?

Coaching the team

Teams can provide an excellent environment for skills development. Groups of people can generate more ideas than individuals, and the atmosphere of a supportive team can help to dispel the threatening sense of being put on the spot. This kind of work, in turn, can strengthen the team itself, renewing its values and redefining its identity.

As team leader, assure them that you aren't forcing them into training against their will. Identify the goals of the coaching session and work to create the non-threatening conditions that allow people to contribute creatively.

Involve the whole team in establishing standards. Ask them how they would recognize an effective work document. You will probably easily agree that it is accurate, clear and easily understandable.

Discuss what you might do to develop these qualities. Use examples of documents to stimulate the conversation. You could start with standard letters and paragraphs, where authorship is less controversial. Move on, perhaps, to your own documents, asking for comments and suggestions. It's important to stress that everybody's work can benefit from other people's ideas. As you move on to examples from team members, try to avoid anonymity. Establish the principle of individual responsibility: every writer must take ownership of their work and any coaching from you or the team is with the agreement of the writer and at their service. Full responsibility for complete pieces of work encourages a more creative and self-motivating approach.

You can offer broader support to the team in a number of ways. Wherever you can, give people challenging tasks: a tricky complaint response, a report that builds the writer's competence or knowledge. We are all energized by work that helps us grow. Build a team culture in which it's as acceptable to ask for advice as to offer it. Lead by example, asking your team for suggestions to improve your own work. Offer advice, but only if it's asked for. Maximize the opportunities for the team to suggest improvements. People should feel comfortable offering – and asking for – ideas. Your role as a manager then becomes the guardian of the standards and the facilitator of productive conversations. Impose solutions as rarely as you can, admitting that you don't have all the answers.

Other ideas for fostering an awareness of good writing include:

- supplying a good dictionary, thesaurus and guide to usage
- circulating newspaper and magazine articles about writing
- publishing your own style guide, including specific standards for clarity
- publicizing letters and other documents that are particularly effective
- giving every member of your team a copy of this book!

THE APPENDICES

These appendices include material that supports the guidance given elsewhere in the book. Inevitably, I have only been able to summarize some essential points of grammar here. For more help, and a far more comprehensive guide to the details of grammar and punctuation, turn to *The Grammar Workbook* by Paul Brollo.

The parts of speech

The parts of speech are the different jobs done by words in sentences. For each part of speech, a few examples follow.

Noun

Nouns identify objects.

Common nouns name ordinary objects:
table, chair, bell, book, candle, pen, car.

Proper nouns are the names we give to specific people, places, months or organizations:
Jane, Toronto, September, The London Stock Exchange.

Collective nouns name groups of people or things. They almost always take a singular verb:
team, company, committee, flock, herd.

Abstract nouns name concepts or qualities: anything that does not exist physically:
usage, management, integration, charity, implementation, agreement.

Gerunds are nouns formed from verbs. They always end in *-ing:*
buying, selling, walking, costing, budgeting, raising.

Pronoun

Stands in place of a noun:
I, you, he, she, it, we, they, which, who, that, anyone, everybody.

Verb

Expresses an action or state of being. Verbs can take many forms, depending on who or what is acting, and tense – the time when the

action takes place:
to run: runs, is running, has run, has been running, will run ...
to be: am, is, are, is being, has been, will be ...

Adjective

Describes a noun or pronoun:
black, large, fine, robust, best, disused, frequent, effective.

Article

An adjective-like word that attaches to a noun. There are three articles in English:
the (definite article)
a (indefinite article before a noun starting with a consonant)
an (indefinite article before a noun starting with a vowel).

Adverb

Modifies a verb, saying how, when, where, or why an action is happening. Adverbs can also modify adjectives, other adverbs or whole clauses:
quickly, directly, readily, costly, only, however, lately, locally.

Conjunction

Joins words, phrases or clauses:
and, but, or, although, while, because, since, if.

Preposition

Precedes a noun or pronoun:
on, by, up, over, between, in, during, for, underneath, with, without.
Any group of words beginning with a preposition is a *prepositional phrase:*
in the sea, between you and me, during the meeting, with a plate of bread and butter.

Interjection

An exclamatory word or phrase:
well, er, no, oh, ugh!

Sentence construction

A sentence is a group of words that makes complete sense by itself. Every sentence must have a *subject* and a *predicate*. The subject is what the sentence is about; the predicate is what we are saying about the subject in the rest of the sentence. The predicate must always contain a verb.

The tenants pay rent monthly.
Subject: *the tenants*
Predicate: *pay rent monthly*
Verb: *pay*

We construct sentences in three main ways.

A *simple sentence* contains one idea:
Many tenants pay rent monthly.

A *compound sentence* joins two simple sentences with a conjunction:
Many tenants pay rent monthly but a few choose to pay every week.

A *complex sentence* adds one or more extra ideas to the main idea. The extra ideas are often surrounded by commas:
Many tenants pay rent monthly, although a few pay weekly.
Many tenants, including some living on income support, pay rent monthly.
Although many are living on income support, our tenants prefer to pay monthly.

Bones of contention

A few issues of grammar and usage arise over and over again in business writing. I've included the most common ones here. To find out more or delve more deeply, I recommend *The Complete Plain Words* by Sir Ernest Gowers (revised Greenbaum and Whitcut) and *The Oxford Guide to English Grammar* by John Eastwood.

I've also been guided in some of these entries by R W Burchfield's remarks in *The New Fowler's Modern English Usage*. On occasions I quote him, with thanks: his words are followed by [RWB].

Abbreviations

Abbreviations may take full stops, but increasingly omit them:
I.o.W./IoW (Isle of Wight)
a.m./am
D.Phil/DPhil.

Familiar abbreviations always omit stops, as do acronyms pronounced as a word:
BBC, OUP, TUC
NATO, Ofwat, Anzac.

Contractions almost always now omit full stops:
Dr, Mr, Ms, St . . .

Plurals of abbreviations may take or omit an apostrophe:
MPs/MP's
CEOs/CEO's.

Establish clear conventions and maintain consistency:
For e.g. and i.e., see under E.g./i.e.

And/But/Because to start sentences

Yes! You *can* start sentences with these words. Using *But* is more common. Placing *And* at the beginning of a sentence creates a more dramatic effect; you may not wish to make such a 'style statement'.

'There is a persistent belief that it is improper to begin a sentence with *And*, but this prohibition has been cheerfully ignored by standard authors from Anglo-Saxon times onward.' [RWB] Similarly with *But*: the widespread belief that this word should never start a sentence, says Burchfield, 'has no foundation'.

These two words are *conjunctions*: their function is to join phrases or sentences and they cannot logically come at the start of a sentence. But, in the murky waters of grammar, logic always loses in the battle with usage. If you don't like putting these words at the beginning of a sentence, do something else.

There is even less reason to prohibit the use of *Because* at the start of a sentence. The word normally introduces a subordinate clause or phrase (*because of . . .*); these can obviously come at the start of the sentence:

Because we have limited space, places on the course are limited.
Because of increased demand, we have had to limit places on the course.

The same principle applies to other conjunctions: *although, while, since* and so on.

Capital letters

Use capital letters:
- to start a sentence
- at the beginning of a passage of direct speech (in speech marks, '. . .')
- for proper nouns (names of specific people, places, things, months and days)
- for adjectives derived from proper nouns: *German, Elizabethan, Chinese*
- for the first and all main words in any kind of title:
  Our Mutual Friend
  Far from the Madding Crowd
  The Antiques Roadshow
  The Independent

The Crown and Greyhound
National Sales Manager
Women's Institute
Archbishop of York

- at the beginning of a line of verse
- for the pronoun *I*.

One of the most common questions concerns job titles. Specific names of jobs take capital letters: *National Sales Manager, Regional Advisor, Assistant Marketing Director.* If you are using the words to indicate a *type* of job, use lower-case letters:

We asked managers to contribute budgets by April.
The company employs consultants to advise on strategy.

Conjunctions to start sentences

See *And/But/Because* to start sentences.

Could/Would/Should

Conventions surrounding these words are extremely complicated and confusing. The most frequent question that arises in business English concerns the construction *I should/would be grateful if you could/would . . . .* In formal standard English, *should* follows *I/we* and *would* follows all other pronouns. Usage suggests that, in the construction quoted here, either can now follow *I/we. Could* has connotations of ability. *Would* probably makes more sense.

A simple solution, in this case, is to cut out the construction altogether. Say *Please* instead.

Dangling participle

A fairly common error. A participle (ending in *-ing*) in a subordinate clause should have a subject:

The lights having gone out, we couldn't see a thing.
(Subject: *lights*)

If there is no subject in the clause, the subject is understood to be the same as in the main clause:

Walking across a field, we saw a plane fly past.
(Subject: *we*)

The danger is that the participle comes to relate to the wrong subject:

Walking across a field, a plane flew past.

(Subject: *a plane*, which cannot walk across a field.)

The mistake arises usually in longer, more complicated sentences:

As a valued member of the swimming scheme, I thought it would be a good idea to inform you of our new training opportunities.

This suggests that *I* am a member of the scheme, which isn't the sense intended. The sentence might read:

As a valued member of the swimming scheme, you will be interested to read about our new training opportunities.

Disagreement between subject and verb

A singular subject must take a singular verb, a plural subject a plural verb:

One of the cats was ill.

A range of goods is available.

Our objectives for the project are too ambitious.

Collective nouns (naming groups of people or things) usually take singular verbs. They can take plural verbs if we want to stress the idea of a group of individuals:

The committee was unanimous in its decision.

The committee were quarrelling for over an hour.

The company is the largest in the county.

All the company were present at the presentation.

E.g./i.e.

E.g. stands for exempli gratia and means 'for example'. I.e. stands for id est, meaning 'that is'.

RWB consistently gives each abbreviation stops as printed here. Eg, ie are also acceptable; eg., ie. are probably not.

Many people confuse these two terms or don't know what they mean. Try to avoid using them. Write 'for example' or 'that is' in full, or find another solution.

Fewer/Less

Few/fewer are used with countable nouns; *less* usually refers to quantity:

Fewer customers were happy with our service this year.

There was less satisfaction recorded with our service this year.

Have/Of

Of is not a verb.

You should have told me about the increased price. [Correct]

You should of told me about the increased price. [Incorrect]

He/She/They

We have a problem in English when we want to talk about a single person whose sex is unknown. Traditional grammarians (nearly all of them men) taught writers to assume that the person was male and to use *he, him, his*. A less sexist approach might result in *he or she, he/she* or even *s/he* – all of which are clumsy.

The OED allows the use of *they* 'used in reference to a singular noun ... applicable to either sex'. Usage has never doubted that anyone can use the word if they want to refer to one person without mentioning their gender. Some people persist in regarding this usage as wrong. The Plain English Campaign, and others of us who would rather not ignore 50% of the human race, disagree.

Everyone should bring their books to the lecture.

Each time a visitor arrives, we should greet them warmly and take their coat.

An alternative is sometimes to put the noun into the plural:

We should greet all visitors warmly and take their coats.

However

Never use *however* as a substitute for *but*.

There is no need for an extra building however the power room must be well ventilated. [Incorrect]

However in this context means 'nevertheless'. The simplest solution is to place it at the start of a new sentence, followed by a comma:

There is no need for an extra building. However, the power room must be well ventilated.

It's/Its

A persistent error.
It's always means either 'It is' or 'It has'.
It's a long way to London from here.
It's been raining hard during the night.
Its is a possessive adjective, like *his, her, their, my, our.*
The dog ate its dinner.
The product is successful and we are committed to its future.

Prepositions at the end of sentences

A preposition logically precedes its noun. The myth (RWB's word) arose in the seventeenth century that prepositions should never, therefore, end a sentence. Don't hesitate to end a sentence with a preposition if your ear tells you to. The alternative is probably awkward and may sound ridiculous.
With what should I use this?
What should I use this with?

Nobody has told me to whom I should report.
Nobody has told me who to report to.

This is a result for which we cannot account.
This is a result we cannot account for. [- or, of course:]
We cannot account for this result.

Churchill apparently once replied to a tortuous memo: 'This is the kind of English up with which I will not put.' Of course, prepositions at the ends of sentences can get out of control. Another well known example quotes a nurse, speaking to a child who has brought her a book: 'What did you bring that book I don't like to be read aloud to out of up for?'

The reason is because . . .

This construction says the same thing twice. You need only write *The reason is that . . .* or *this is because.*

-Self/-selves

Words ending thus are reflexive pronouns. We mainly use them:

- when the subject is also the object of the action (*I cut myself gardening*); or
- for emphasis (*I can do it myself*).

Take care not to use these words when the simple pronoun will do.

It was a pleasure to meet yourself. [Incorrect]

It was a pleasure to meet you.

Split infinitives

Perhaps the most infamous of grammatical issues. The infinitive of the verb *to go* can be split by an adverb or adverbial phrase: *to boldly go* is surely the most celebrated split infinitive in history.

Argument has raged over this issue for at least a hundred years. Clearly, many people still feel strongly that to split the infinitive is 'wrong'. Equally, following the non-splitting rule rigidly can lead to awkwardness. Splitting an infinitive with a single word is hardly a sin, though some readers may object. 'Avoid splitting infinitives whenever possible, but do not feel undue remorse if a split infinitive is unavoidable for the natural ... completion of a sentence.' [RWB].

For your safety we ask you to please stay in your seats.

That's where you have to really watch yourself.

Falling sales led the company to finally abandon the Asian market.

Distribution systems have to radically change.

Splitting an infinitive with an adverbial phrase may create an ugly effect:

Everything she said seemed to just deliberately and maliciously criticize our policy.

Everything she said seemed only deliberate and malicious criticism of our policy.

That

That is an awkward word because it can be a conjunction, a pronoun or an adjective.

I think that I have a meeting on Friday. [Conjunction]

The box that you want is on the top shelf. [Relative pronoun]

That doesn't make sense. [Demonstrative pronoun]
He agreed to send that paper in the next post. [Adjective]

In the first two cases, the word could be taken out. In the last two, it could not. I prefer to use the conjunction *that* rather than risk misunderstanding by removing it. But using it more than once in a sentence is usually unnecessary.

I think that the equipment that he wants is in that corner.
I think the equipment he wants is in that corner.

Which/That

These relative pronouns are often confused. A useful distinction is to see *that* as defining and *which* as non-defining. In other words, *that* specifies the noun it relates to and *which* adds descriptive detail.

I wrote this article with a pen that my partner bought me in Lisbon. [Specifies or identifies the pen]

I wrote this article with a pen, which my partner bought me in Lisbon. [Adds detailed description about the pen]

Many writers don't observe or recognize this distinction; and there are many instances when it is hard to decide which kind of clause you are writing.

Words often confused

The following are the most common confusions surrounding similar words. If in doubt, use a dictionary.

Accept/Except

To *accept* is to receive with thanks or assent. To *except* is to leave out or exclude. *Except*, of course, can also mean 'not including'.
I accept that you may not be able to finish by Thursday.
Nobody can be excepted from this general rule.
Everybody except Gerald has hit their targets.

Affect/Effect

Affect is normally a verb, meaning 'to influence'.
Effect is usually a noun, meaning 'the result of an action'.
It can also be a verb, meaning 'to bring into being'.
The decision will affect all subsequent operations.
The economic situation has had an adverse effect on our business.
We have not been able to effect an improvement in quality.

Complement/Compliment

Complement is a noun meaning 'that which makes up or completes' or a verb meaning 'to complete or form a fitting companion to'.
Compliment is a noun meaning 'praise' or the verb meaning 'to praise'.
The team needs a full complement of players to qualify.
It costs nothing to pay somebody a compliment.

Dependant/Dependent

Dependant is a noun: 'a person depending on another'.

Dependent is an alternative spelling, according to *The Chambers Dictionary* (though not according to Gowers). It is also an adjective meaning 'depending, relying on'.

All staff must ensure that their dependants leave the country by Friday.

We were all dependent on the train leaving on time.

Note that the newspaper, *The Independent*, uses an adjective as part of its name.

Disinterested/Uninterested

To be *disinterested* is to be unbiased. To be *uninterested* is to take no interest.

My neighbour gave a disinterested opinion on the proposed colour scheme.

My daughter was uninterested in doing her homework.

Due to/Owing to

Owing to is a prepositional phrase. *Due* is an adjective and cannot, say some, be used otherwise. Strictly, then, these sentences are correct.

The trains were late owing to signalling problems.

The lateness of the trains was due to signalling problems.

But these are not.

The trains were late due to signalling problems.

The lateness of the trains was owing to signalling problems.

The general patterns are: 'This happened owing to that' and 'This was due to that.'

In truth, many (most?) of us now cannot see or hear the distinction, and the two phrases are coming to mean the same thing. If in doubt, use *because of*. Both of these examples are correct.

The trains were late because of signalling problems.

The lateness of the trains was because of signalling problems.

Ensure/Insure

To *ensure* is to make sure; to *insure* is to pay money to protect something.

I ensured that all the doors were locked.

He told me to insure my jewellery.

Imply/Infer

To *imply* is to suggest indirectly. To *infer* is to understand or derive.
He implied that women were unsuitable for the work.
We infer from what he said that he feels women to be inferior.

Impracticable/Unpracticable

The two words both mean 'not able to be done, lacking feasibility'.
Impracticable is more common. *Impractical,* meaning 'not practical',
seems to me to mean virtually the same but also has the added mean-
ing of 'having an unrealistic approach' in relation to a person.
It was impracticable to fit the equipment into such a small space.
Richard is impractical and could hardly mend an electric plug.

Practice/Practise

Practice is a noun; *to practise* is the verb. Confusion sometimes arises
because American spells both noun and verb *practice.*
The doctor's practice was full.
My music teacher told me to practise each day.

Principal/Principle

Principal can be an adjective, meaning 'first in importance', or a noun,
meaning 'a person first in importance, usually the head teacher in a
school or college'.
Principle is a noun, meaning 'a fundamental truth or idea'.
The principal item on the agenda is the extension to the office building.
The principal welcomed all the parents of new pupils.
One of our guiding principles is respect for everybody in the team.

Some notes on dictation

The golden rule of dictation is:

Put yourself in the typist's place.

Dictation saves time and makes use of valuable secretarial skills (for those of us who don't have to produce our own work!). Because it involves less physical work, you produce words more directly and, usually, more quickly. Because you are speaking, your text has a better chance of being more natural, lively and personal – making it easier to understand.

Effective dictation requires careful planning and thorough editing. You need a clear picture of the whole document before you start. And you must take time to rewrite your draft for accuracy, brevity and clarity.

For the typist, the main problems are:
- ignorance of the subject matter
- lack of familiarity with words and technical terms
- hearing the content only once
- inferior quality of sound
- not knowing the speaker (a temporary typist, perhaps)
- lack of information with the tape
- no instructions – or too many instructions – or confusing instructions.

Get to know your dictating machine. Make sure the recording light is on before you speak. Regularly check the quality of batteries and tapes (a tape will last twice as long if you regularly alternate use of the two sides). Switch it off after use. Keep it clean and well protected.

Plan what you want to say before you start. Make notes or an outline to help you.

- Work out the paragraph structure you wish to use and make sure you indicate paragraph breaks while speaking.
- Keep your sentences as short as possible. You will tend to speak much longer sentences than are comfortable for a reader.
- Send any other documents that will save you dictating: previous correspondence, papers containing names and addresses, product names, reference numbers and so on.
- Make sure you know how to refer accurately to any standard paragraphs the typist may have available.

Give clear instructions at the start of the tape.
- Greet the typist, say who you are and indicate the number of documents on the tape.
- Explain the format of the document: letter, memo, report, any other standard format that the typist will know. Specify the layout if it is unusual in any way. It could be useful to indicate the rough length of the document.
- Specify the number of copies needed, and who should receive them.
- Indicate the heading of the document.

While dictating:
- keep the machine at an even distance from your mouth
- speak in a natural voice at slightly slower than normally speed
- use tone to indicate feeling and emphasis
- play back during recording and check how you sound
- spell unfamiliar words: technical terms, names
- specify the punctuation.

And don't:
- mumble
- speak too fast or slowly
- lapse into colloquial language at the expense of clarity
- think aloud
- eat, smoke or drink
- shout or whisper
- ask the typist to do too much cutting and pasting.

When editing your first draft, pay particular attention to spellings, punctuation, long sentences and unnecessary words.

Where to go from here

Essential books

Brollo, Paul: *The Grammar Workbook*. The Industrial Society, 1999.

Burchfield, RW (ed.): *The New Fowler's Modern English Usage*. Oxford University Press, 1996.

The Chambers Dictionary. Chambers, 1994.

Cutts, Martin: *The Plain English Guide*. Oxford University Press, 1995.

Eastwood, John: *Oxford Guide to English Grammar*. Oxford University Press, 1994.

Gowers, Sir Ernest (revised Greenbaum and Whitcut): *The Complete Plain Words*. HMSO, 1986.

Roget's Thesaurus. Various publishers, including Penguin.